CW00693013

TOMATOES FOR EVERYONE

including Ring Culture and
growing on Straw Bales

Tomatoes for Everyone

including Ring Culture and growing on Straw Bales

by

FRANK W. ALLERTON
B.Sc.Hort.(London); Dip.Hort.(Wye); A.R.I.C.

with a foreword by

FRED STREETER
A.H.R.H.S., V.M.H.

FABER AND FABER
London · Boston

First published in 1956
by Faber and Faber Limited
3 Queen Square London WC1
First published in this edition 1971
Reprinted 1973, 1975, and 1980
Printed in Great Britain by
Whitstable Litho Ltd., Whitstable, Kent
All rights reserved

ISBN 0 571 09749 9 (Faber Paperbacks)
ISBN 0 571 04615 0 (hard bound edition)

FOREWORD

It was a joy to know that my old friend Frank Allerton has had so much success with *Tomatoes for Everyone* since it was published close on ten years ago that this revised and up-to-the-minute edition has been asked for.

Now we have straw-bale growing to challenge the long success of ring culture which Mr. Allerton introduced and we can expect even heavier crops of the finest quality.

When I think back over seventy-five years of gardening and remember all the work we put into growing tomatoes, it makes one think how scientific advances have helped the gardener. Tomatoes are produced by the ton on straw beds and the new chapter on this method will help thousands of amateurs with little greenhouses to be just as successful.

I get many queries on the use of straw bales and now we have all the answers!

Just imagine what it means to grow your own fruit—and what a saving besides the enjoyment of real home-grown flavour!

I strongly advise you to get this book and follow the simple instructions. I only wish I had been able to obtain a copy years ago!

Foreword

Mr. Allerton has made a study of tomatoes all his life and here is a great chance for you to benefit by his latest writings. I wish the new edition every success.

Fred Streeter

CONTENTS

9

ILLUSTRATIONS

PREFACE

O f all the food plants we grow in garden, allotment or greenhouse, the tomato inspires, I think, the most general interest. The reasons are not far to seek.

In the first place, it is an alien plant which has become nearly, but not quite, a native of our climate. For this reason, it requires a certain skill to grow it to perfection and therein lies the challenge which few with the spirit of the land in their veins can resist.

Again, it has the solid worth of a vegetable combined with the more elegant qualities of a fruit and, moreover, it has become so staple an article of diet that few must be the households that do not enjoy its virtues in many forms.

Add to these undeniable qualities those of a handsome habit of growth which makes it acceptable beyond the earthy confines of the vegetable plot, an established commercial value and a health-giving food, and we have very sound reasons for the gardeners' unusual interest.

But what of this challenge to skill? Why do so few gardeners manage to provide the household tomato requirements except, perhaps, in the autumn when interest in salad meals is waning?

Therein lies the main purpose of this book. To set forth as gardener to gardeners the skill and contrivance required for effective outdoor culture and to show how, even in the less favourable summers, everyone can produce *ripe* tomatoes, not as an autumn glut but in steady and worth-while supply from early August onwards.

The chapter on greenhouse culture shows how the outdoor crop may be preceded by several weeks with only the most modest expenditure in fuel. In view of the multitude of purposes for which the gardener requires his greenhouse, a special point is made of the way in which a crop of tomatoes can be taken between the end of the general propagating season and the housing of the Late-flowering chrysanthemums.

For ease of reference, separate chapters are devoted to such subjects as obtaining and preparing the soil for the containers, pest and disease control, feeding and varieties. An appendix is included for tabular information and to allow more complete information on brief references in the text.

Several mentions of ring culture appear in the text since experience over a number of years shows that this system of growing is not only capable of producing heavy crops of high quality but also overcomes the difficult amateur problem of disease-ridden greenhouse soil. My companion book, *Ring Culture*, covers this system in full detail while for a more fundamental approach to culture in general I would suggest reference to *Tomato Growing*. Both are published by Faber & Faber.

For this revised edition, a chapter on the interesting new straw-bale method of growing has been included.

Chapter 1

OUTDOOR CULTURE: SITE AND SYSTEM

It is generally accepted in commercial circles that, except in favoured southern areas, the outdoor tomato crop is a gamble with the grower at the winning end scarcely more than one season in four. The weight of ripe, sound fruit, the proportion of the various grades of quality and the average price per grade all come into the picture when one is setting cost of production and handling against market returns.

As gardeners our picture is simpler; cost of production and market value mean little. On the other hand, we are very much concerned with the weight of ripe fruit produced and with quality. We must admit also that, if we are able to supply our own needs when the price in the shops is around 40p. per lb., the sense of achievement is greater than with a plentiful supply in the autumn when 20p. per lb. is nearer the figure.

Now, if under garden or allotment conditions the tomato crop could not be made more reliable than in the field, it would scarcely warrant the trouble of preparing the land and planting. The fact that a worth-while crop of ripe fruit can, with a little contrivance, be produced even in unfavourable seasons such as 1954, provides the justification for this book.

By 'contrivance' I mean making the very best use of the protection against the cold winds and early and late season frosts which is afforded naturally by walls and fences and which can

13

be augmented by various simple means; by the use of some form of container raised above the surrounding soil level and by employing ring culture or straw-bale culture.

All this may sound formidable and very much of a specialist approach but, in fact, it involves nothing more than using, or making, a 'warm corner' and employing simple methods based on modern plant research to ensure strong, rapid and fruitful growth irrespective of the fertility or otherwise of the garden soil.

Certainly, no matter how or where we plant, the right type of plant, ready at the right time, is a prime essential but it will make for simplicity if we work step by step with the calendar and let propagation or the purchase of plants fall into logical sequence. Now we are at the end of the season; the first frosts have cut down the tender plants—including the tomatoes—and there is time in hand to prepare for next year. First of all then:

THE SITE

I well remember, as a schoolboy down near the coast in East Kent, my grandfather growing his tomatoes against the south end of the old black-tarred garden shed wherein he kept, and guarded with piercing eye and heavy hand, his accumulated treasures. Alongside the shed and, indeed, surrounding the whole garden, was a great thick hedge of elderberry which defied even the searching east winds of that exposed district.

The spot was a suntrap; the black shed boards sucked in the heat to release it again in the cool of the night and the old man grew there tomatoes which, even allowing for the glamour of the past warping one's memory, were the earliest and finest and the best flavoured in the village. Even his neighbours admitted that Grandfather could grow 'maters and that—if you know village life—is quite something!

14

Outdoor Culture: Site and System

The point I am making is that the site chosen for growing tomatoes out of doors is all-important. Bear in mind that here we have a native of the Mediterranean area where springs are soft and lush and summers hot and dry. Throughout most of the British Isles, away from the protection of walls and fences and shed-ends and so on, the night air in the early summer is too chill to permit steady growth and free-setting of the blooms. Often tomatoes planted in a row across the kitchen garden or allotment scarcely commence to grow before mid-July, and the first fruit has not reached the stage of maturity needed for colouring much before early September.

To serve our purpose of producing tomatoes out of doors while they are still dear enough in the shops to be really worth growing, we must set aside the warmest, most sheltered corner of the garden and, if no solid fence or wall exists, a north and east background protection, at least 3 ft. 6 in. in height, must be contrived. This may take the form of overlapped weather-boarding or boards closely butted to prevent the chill draughts which tender plants dislike so much. Wood in some form is best as, being a good insulator, it maintains a more even daytime temperature and radiates heat for a longer period at night than corrugated iron or other metal. Failing wood, however, a metal or asbestos sheeting 'wall' is certainly better than an open site.

An erection of 4-inch breeze blocks provides, of course, the ideal conditions, but few gardeners would be prepared to erect so permanent a structure for tomato growing.

On the allotment, old corrugated iron sheeting is perhaps the most convenient material for making a cheap and easily erected north and east enclosure but straw bales, later to be used for composting, provide the most effective of all 'rough' shelter. Beware of slugs, snails and woodlice if these are used, however!

Since we are concerned with trapping as much early season sun-heat as possible, a dark background surface is desirable. Creosote applied some months before planting is a satisfactory

15

treatment for wood, while agricultural bitumen paint serves for metal or asbestos sheeting. With straw bale walls the only practical method of darkening is to dust liberally with old soot which, incidentally, also serves the purpose of deterring pests.

The whole purpose of the background is to increase the prevailing temperatures around the plants in the early season, and the mere fact of breaking the cold winds does much towards this end.

Though it might be obvious, it should perhaps be emphasized that the protective background should be mainly on the north side with the projection for at least 2 ft. on the east side to break winds from that quarter. In the case of a dwelling-house with a fence or wall running roughly east and west, the corner made by house and fence is obviously the ideal spot as far as warmth and shelter are concerned.

METHOD OF GROWING

As a rule, whether one is planting against a protective background or out in the open, the soil on the spot is thoroughly prepared beforehand by digging, or double-digging if necessary, and by working in compost heap material or stable manure supplemented with a base fertilizer. A note on soil preparation is given in the Appendix.

Certainly this obvious way of going to work has the justification of long-established practice, and it gives good results in those hot, dry summers which seem these days to be the exception rather than the rule.

Under less favourable conditions, however, and especially with a lack of sun in the early season, the coldness of the ground limits root growth and prevents the quick establishment of the plants so essential if early maturity is to be achieved. For this reason, it is better to plant in some form of container

16

which, in effect, raises the roots above the general soil level and thus allows quicker penetration of the sun's heat.

A great variety of containers can be made to serve our purpose and I have used everything from 9-inch clay pots to deep boxes with excellent results. An illustration shows canteen-size fruit tins used to good purpose, and the stronger types of waterproofed cardboard or composition pots now generally available at garden shops are ideal for one season of growth.

Cement pots, which are becoming available as cheaper, though more cumbersome, substitutes for 'clays', are also suitable, and in fact almost any container which is provided with a drainage hole or holes and which will hold about 14 lb. of a soil compost can be made to serve.

In my experience, some form of container is a great advantage in producing an early crop and the expense involved for a dozen or two plants is not prohibitive even if 'cardboards' have to be purchased.

Now having decided upon which type of container suits one's convenience or pocket, it remains to employ them to the best purpose.

There are four possibilities. The first involves standing the containers on the border soil which has previously been deeply cultivated, manured and fertilized. The second applies where it is desired to grow the crop against a wall bordered by a hard path or concrete surface. In this instance the roots are, by force of circumstances, restricted to the container and the entire food and water supply of the plant is dependent upon the container compost.

The third is ring culture, a system which I developed, and introduced, to gardeners a number of years ago. So successful and popular has this system proved to be that I have devoted a companion book to it, as detailed in the Preface.

Finally, there is the new straw-bale method of growing developed at the Lee Valley Experimental Horticultural Station and this, while primarily intended for under-glass growing, can be employed to good purpose in the garden. Chapter 6 covers the practical details of this method.

Chapter 2

OUTDOOR CULTURE: THE GROWING SEASON

S pring has arrived and now, with April days passing the half-way mark, we are scheduled to plant in the containers. Schedules are necessary even with gardening, but the weather is always the deciding factor. It should, according to season, be a mellow combination of showers, soft breezes and ever-warmer sunshine. In fact, it is just as likely to be blowing a gale or snowing.

Faced with unseasonably cold or rough weather, we have no option but to wait. If the plants have been booked at the local nursery and calls on space prevent their being held for a few days, they can be transported in a deep, covered box—a desirable protection in any case—and stood on the window-ledge of an unheated room. A piece of hardboard will protect the ledge and, if the plants are in pots, they can be stood out practically touching. If soil blocks have been used, the roots would tend to be checked in the relatively dry atmosphere and it is advisable to stand the blocks in seed trays and surround them with moistened peat.

If the plants have not been as well hardened off as they should be, they may show their dislike of the lower temperature by curling and down-turning of the leaves, but this is only a temporary condition and need cause no concern. The pots or boxes should be turned each day and, providing the soil does not dry out, the less water applied to the roots the less will the plants suffer from indoor conditions.

The more fortunate gardener who is raising his own plants, whether it be in a greenhouse, heated frame or nothing more extensive than a home propagator of the type described in Chapter 4, can tide over a period of unfavourable planting weather and can combine hardening off with continued steady growth.

In the meantime, the compost (potting soil) should be tipped out of the boxes or sacks and given another turn, as it tends to become 'lifeless' if stored for more than a fortnight or so without aeration.

Just as soon as the weather allows, the job of planting should go ahead and I find the following procedure as simple and effective as any: containers of the chosen type are lined up close to the site and a heap or barrow-load of the compost is provided. A tile or asbestos sheet a foot or so square is placed level on the ground and one of the bottomless containers stood upon it. Compost is now filled in loosely nearly to the top and an empty clay pot of the exact size in which the plants are growing is pushed into the centre of the compost down to the rim and the compost worked down firmly round the sides with a blunt piece of stick. Further compost is added as required until finally the pot can be withdrawn leaving a firm block of compost in the container and a cavity of the correct shape, but a trifle larger than a turned-out ball of roots. Where the plants are in soil blocks, a piece of wood of slightly greater diameter and roughly the right shape should be used instead of an empty pot to form the cavity.

Providing the compost has been prepared from soil which is nicely moist but not wet, from well-moistened but not saturated peat and dry sand of the correct grade, it will stand this light ramming without becoming a sticky, air-less mass. A firm root-run is essential if growth is to be steady and fruitful and, to achieve the right condition with light ramming, the texture of the compost when filled into the containers should be such that a handful firmly squeezed will adhere but will fall apart when lightly pressed or dropped from a height of a couple of feet or so.

The final level of the compost in the container, incidentally, should be about 1½ inches below the rim as sufficient room must be left for watering as the season progresses.

At this stage, the filled containers must be transferred to their permanent site in a row close to the protecting background.

Where the border soil has been prepared for later penetration of the roots from the containers, or a ring culture 'trough' has been arranged, the procedure is to lift the container by means of the tile and place it squarely upon the border soil or aggregate in the trough. The tile is now drawn out carefully to leave the container standing squarely upon the soil or aggregate. Whatever the system adopted, a suitable spacing for the containers—from centre to centre—is 15 inches for any but the most vigorous and leafy varieties, and these justify 18-inch spacing.

Planting can now proceed. The plants, watered the day before to ensure thoroughly moist but not sticky soil, are turned out one at a time by placing the fingers across the soil surface, inverting the pot and striking the rim sharply on the edge of a firm object such as a box.

At this stage, one can judge the quality of the plant by the amount and colour of the roots. The ball of compost turned out of the pot should have a surrounding sheath of glistening white roots with no trace of browning or decay. The top growth should, ideally, be short-jointed and thick-set, with a dense mat of shiny hairs on the stem and the two seed leaves or cotyledons still firm and bright green. The height from the pot surface will be 6–9 inches and the first truss will be just visible when the growing point is gently parted. Far less perfect plants, however, can be relied upon to do well and the most important point to look for is a clean, vigorous root system. From experience, I would much rather have hard, blue-green plants with abundant healthy roots than those with luxuriant tops and only a few weak roots showing round the ball of compost. The former will grow away rapidly given half a chance; the latter frequently stand still for a fortnight or more while making the roots which, under forcing conditions, they could not make during the propagating period.

The plants are transferred to the prepared cavities in the containers with no more disturbance of the roots than is necessary to remove the pieces of drainage crocks, where, indeed, these have been used.

With J.I. compost, the texture is so favourable to drainage that in the 3-inch pots commonly used for propagating no such crocking is required.

Now, as explained, the cavity is slightly larger than the turned-out ball of root and this means that the neck of the plant stands a little below the compost level in the container and that there is a small gap all round. This gap is now filled by running in a little of the compost which has been passed through a $\frac{1}{4}$ inch sieve specially for this purpose. This same compost is used to level-up the surface of the compost, and the plant is settled by light pressure with the fingers.

The result is a plant with about $\frac{1}{2}$ inch of the previously exposed stem covered by new compost. This is a desirable procedure since the tomato is one of those plants which readily produces roots from the base of the stem. These should be encouraged as the more vigorously and quickly the root system can be established in the containers the better will be the chance of early fruit as well as a lasting crop. At this stage no water should be given as both the ball of roots and the new compost are moist and our aim is to encourage the roots to

22

work into the new compost in search of water and food rather than to restrict the need for extension by applying water near the stem.

Although we are concerned with growing an outdoor crop, there is an excuse at this stage for cheating to an extent by giving the additional protection of a modified form of cloche. One could, of course, stand the high-barn type of cloche over the containers in a complete row and fill the ends with sheets of glass. It is a simple and effective way, but by no means every gardener has these fairly expensive types available and, if he has, they are probably being used already for early salad crops in the vegetable garden.

It will be apparent that we do not need a complete cloche but rather a sheet of glass standing vertically or sloping slightly inwards a few inches in front of the containers and extending some inches above the plants and, connected to this, an upward sloping sheet resting against the protecting wall or other structure. It so happens that a special type of clamp with carrying handle combined is available for assembling the various types of cloche to take the place of the usual supporting wires. The angles at which the clamps are set correspond to the ridge or the side junction as the case may be and the latter suits our purpose admirably.

As the sheets of glass need to be fairly large—15 inches square or some similar standard size—two clamps to each half cloche may prove desirable to take the weight. It is a good plan to support the roof glass at the back with a narrow shelf of wood fixed at appropriate height to the protecting structure. In this way a continuous 'tunnel' of glass is provided at minimum cost and the ends can be blocked by sheets of glass or even pieces of asbestos board.

It is also advisable, incidentally, to push a cane firmly into the ground immediately in front of each half cloche to prevent any tragedies in rough weather. Alternatively, if one wants to

23

be extra careful, a peg can be driven into the soil in front of each and a string carried up to be looped to a nail in the protecting structure at the back. Where a concrete or hard path surface is concerned, a brick in front of each will effectively replace the peg.

This extra protection of the glass enables the plants to withstand a spell of cold spring weather without being seriously checked.

In the event of anything unusually extreme or where the nights are really cold, it is worth going to the bother of covering the glass with hessian or thin sacking at nightfall. A convenient way of doing this is to secure strips of the material to the wall or fence behind in order that it may hang down over the glass. The front of each strip can be held to the ground with a large stone or a brick and during the daytime the strips can be rolled up and tied back to the wall or fence.

One can, if the plants are being grown in a convenient place near the house, go one stage further and place a mains voltage soil-heating cable along the row of containers and double back, if required, to make use of the full length of the cable. The expenditure in electricity is very small even if the cable is kept on continuously for some days, and this small amount of heat makes a surprising difference in periods when the expected warmth from the sun is not forthcoming. Admittedly, however, this is going to rather an extreme of refinement and one can certainly get good results without artificial heat in anything like a normal season.

Just how long the plants should be covered by glass and how soon they will need the first watering depends entirely on the weather. In a favourable season where there has been a good deal of early sunshine, the plants will have increased several times in size by the middle of May and will be almost touching the glass.

At this stage, the half cloches should be moved apart to

leave about an inch gap between each to accustom the plants to full ventilation and, by the end of May, the glass can be removed altogether.

I have dealt with this question of protection from glass in some detail, since it is most useful for bringing the plants on early, but I would emphasize that with plants thoroughly hardened-off before planting, it is optional in warm springs. Without this extra protection the plants may look thoroughly miserable and grow very little in a cold spell, but it takes unusually hard conditions for that time of the year to do any real harm.

Now to return to the question of watering. Within reason, the longer one can withhold water the more effectively will the roots establish in the container compost. There comes a time, however, a fortnight or so after planting, when the compost is looking distinctly dry on top and is beginning to shrink slightly from the sides of the container. This is the sign for watering to commence, but it is advisable to go easy and to stop short of supplying sufficient water to soak the compost right through.

The plants would love a real soaking, but they would probably respond by making unduly soft growth. It is better to apply only a pint or so to each container and to repeat the dose a few days later, and so on, in order to hold the roots back somewhat and thereby apply a degree of the control on the vigour of growth which is possible only in containers.

By habit the tomato is trailing rather than stiffly upright in growth and, if left to its own devices, tends to form a low-growing, bushy plant. This tendency for branching appears quite early and is fully apparent by the time that growth becomes free. Thus, early in June, when the bottom truss should be at the setting stage, an untrimmed plant would have side shoots several inches long.

While this is a desirable feature with the bush varieties which have been specially bred for low branching growth, it must be counteracted where we require the plant to extend vertically with the support of a cane or string. For this reason, side shoots must be removed as soon as they are 2 inches or so long and can be snapped out cleanly by bending them sideways from the stem. It should be remembered that these side shoots are poaching the strength which should be directed entirely into the production of fruit and extension growth, as a single stem. Trimming, i.e. removal of all side growths should be a regular weekly operation and one can either use a sharp knife with due care to avoid leaving a stump to decay or snap the shoots away when they are stiff and turgid in the morning or evening. I, personally, prefer the snapping method as it can leave no 'snag' to decay, and the potential danger of a slipping knife is avoided.

One sometimes finds that the newcomer to tomato growing is so concerned with doing the right thing and removing these side shoots before they can draw on the strength of the plant that he tries to remove them with the tip of a penknife as soon as they are visible. This is not wise, as with succulent young growth, it is all too easy to injure the main stem. Furthermore, it is not necessary because the effects of the side growths are not felt until they become quite large and, indeed, some experienced growers maintain that these shoots increase the effective leaf area of the young plant and therefore should not be removed too soon.

It will be found, incidentally, that though a shoot arises in each leaf axil, i.e. where each leaf joins the main stem, a much stronger one than usual grows out from the axil of the leaf which is immediately below a truss. It is as though the stem, having produced a truss, tends to pass on the job of extension growth to some degree to this side shoot. If it were retained, however, the main shoot would not in fact stop growing but a plant with a double 'leader' would result.

It is better not to allow this to happen even if extra room between each plant is allowed, since this virtually double plant is a big strain for one root system to support. It is an interesting experiment, nevertheless, and, if all goes well, one plant given sufficient space for two leaders will produce almost as much fruit as two separate plants.

As soon as the protecting glass is removed, or right from the time of planting if this extra protection is not afforded, it will be necessary to give some form of support to prevent wind damage. I personally favour strong, soft string for this purpose, and a suitable type is known in the trade as '4-ply Fillis'.

The job is known as 'stringing' and is carried out as follows: One end of the string is secured to the plant itself beneath a leaf using an open loop at least double the size of the stem and secured with a non-slip knot, such as the bowline. The string is then taken up to a taut wire or to a 4-inch nail driven firmly into the wall or fence near the top, and secured by means of a running half-hitch in a condition just taut but without any tendency for pulling on the plant. The plant itself is now twisted round the string in a clockwise direction, care being taken to avoid damaging the leaves or flower trusses. As growth progresses, this procedure is repeated so that no more than 6 inches or so of the stem at the top is ever loose from the string.

This job is best carried out during the daytime and before watering, as the growth is then pliable and will not tend to snap when handled, as it would in the cool of the morning or evening.

It is important, incidentally, not to twist the stem so often that the string passes directly under each leaf axil or a strangled, somewhat corkscrew-like growth will result.

As the plants develop the roots take hold of the compost to an increasing degree and more and more water will be required. It is important not to keep the plants too much on the dry side once they are obviously well established, since the blooms do not set well under dry conditions.

To promote further this setting process, it is a good plan to spray the plants over with water in the morning on warm, sunny days, and it is beneficial to repeat the application in the cool of the evening after a hot day.

If the plants are being grown by ring culture the increasing water requirements are catered for by starting the daily drench of the aggregate. This encourages the formation of water roots in the aggregate, and at the same time keeps the compost moist by suction of water from beneath.

Where the containers are standing on prepared border soil a thorough soaking of the border should now be given to encourage the roots down and sufficient water should be applied in the containers to keep the compost uniformly moist. The difference here is that the compost is less able to draw moisture by suction from soil than from ring culture aggregate.

This need for additional water applies equally to straw-bale culture where, it will be noted, it is essential to keep the straw continually in the thoroughly moist condition achieved by the preparatory soaking.

If all has gone well, the fruits on the bottom truss should be swelling up to walnut size or larger by the end of June and the plants will be a good 2 feet high.

Now comes a critical time, because the operation of feeding to supplement the food supplies in the compost must be commenced. This subject is fully discussed in Chapter 7.

Feeding can usually be continued with advantage until the middle of September to help swell and ripen the higher trusses of fruit. Only in exceptional seasons does the weather remain open far into October and, with falling night temperatures and the normal end-of-season decline in growth, later feeding is unnecessary and, indeed, wasteful.

With this type of protected outdoor cultivation I have found it possible to ripen four trusses completely and the best part of the fifth truss even under the rather cool summers of the last year or two. By the middle of August it has been possible to visualize how many trusses would mature and the plants have been stopped at the seventh truss. This limitation of further extension growth has the result of turning all the energy of growth into maturing the fruit, but even then around 1 lb. per plant of green fruit at various stages of maturity has remained when the first frost brings an end to the season.

One could, of course, stop the plants at the sixth truss, but there is always the hope that there will be a really warm autumn and, at the worst, green fruit can be ripened off gradually indoors or used for chutney.

Stopping, incidentally, involves nothing more than cutting off the head of the plant one leaf above the truss chosen to be the last of the season. As a general guide, it is not worth retaining after mid-August trusses where the first set fruits are smaller than a walnut.

After stopping, vigorous side shoots often appear and, in theory, these should be removed as usual while still small. In practice, however, it is better to allow three or four leaves to develop and then pinch out the growing points. This has the effect of diverting some of the sap which, if left entirely to the fruit, would be likely to cause splitting at the ripening stage.

Some growers strip off the lower leaves as the fruit on adjacent trusses commences to ripen with the idea that the fruit is thus exposed to the sun and so will ripen more quickly. This is a fallacy, because speed of ripening, once maturity has been reached, is conditioned by prevailing temperatures and not by direct sunlight.

Direct sun on the fruit causes overheating and the normal red colour of ripening is replaced by a blotchy orange-yellow. 'Green-back', a hard, green ring at the stalk end, may also occur.

I prefer, then, to retain all foliage as long as it remains green and healthy. Under good conditions of culture, including adequate pest and disease control where necessary, healthy leaves may be hanging down near the containers when one is picking fruit on the fourth truss 3 or 4 feet above.

To summarize, the general cultural routine involves carefully controlled watering of the containers until the roots are allowed to extend below; copious watering of the aggregate or border, and occasional watering in the containers thereafter; twisting the plants periodically for support; removal of all side shoots; feeding; stopping to assist maturity of the last truss; and, throughout, attention to keeping the plants free of pests and disease attack as detailed in Chapter 8.

Chapter 3

THE CONTAINER COMPOST

Whichever way the containers are employed it is easy to appreciate that the rooting medium used therein will largely determine the success or otherwise of the crop.

Thus, where the containers remain throughout the season on a hard surface, both nutrients and water must be supplied entirely by the container compost. Where the plant is ultimately allowed to root through into the border but is restricted for a period with a tile, the formative stage of the crop is dependent upon this relatively small amount of compost and, where ring culture is adopted, the container or 'ring' compost is completely responsible for the nutrient supply of the plant. Only when the container stands direct upon the border soil or on fertilized straw from the first has the plant any chance of being able to overcome the effects of unsuitable container compost. Even then, weak root action in the container may virtually prevent any effective penetration into the border beneath and, at best, the advantages of using a container are largely sacrificed.

So, if we are going to strive after early cropping by using containers we cannot logically be casual about the rooting medium. Granted this, what properties are required in ten container compost?

First and foremost, the ability to promote and maintain strong root action. Unless the roots of any plant are well

31

developed and fully active throughout the growing period, the uptake of both water and nutrients must fall short of what the plant could use.

Secondly, those roots must be sufficiently supplied with both water and nutrients in the right balance to enable the maximum requirements of the plant to be satisfied. Now, this property ranks equal with the first in actual importance as far as the plant is concerned but, when preparing the container compost, it can take second place because the food supply to the plant can be dealt with in stages by growing season feeding whereas the container compost either has the property of promoting and maintaining strong roots from the beginning or it never has.

Fortunately for us gardeners, most of the guesswork in this matter of providing a suitable rooting medium or compost has been eliminated by the classic work over the years of Lawrence and Newell of the John Innes Horticultural Institution. For the best part of thirty years growers—amateur and commercial— have been using their recommended mixtures of fibrous loam, high grade horticultural peat and coarse, sharp sand with first-rate results for a wide range of plants, including tomatoes.

Essentially the John Innes Seed (J.I.S.) and John Innes Potting (J.I.P.) Composts are media designed for just this purpose of promoting and maintaining strong roots. No previous composts so consistently satisfied this primary requirement, and the fact that work on the nutrient levels of composts led to the development of J.I. Base Fertilizer is mainly noteworthy because, again for the first time, the all-important aspect of *balanced* nutrition from the compost, as apart from later feeding, was rationalized.

The John Innes Potting Compost, to which has been added three doses of J.I. Base and of chalk (carbonate of lime), i.e. J.I.P.3, suits our purpose admirably and we have the option of buying it by the bushel ready mixed from specialists in soils and

The quality fruit of *Moneymaker*

Moneymaker again—a market crop in an unheated glasshouse

Ring culture at an early stage

A late-planted crop in a small house. Leaves removed
around mature crop to promote air circulation

The Container Compost

composts or of starting from scratch and making up a soil mixture which embodies at least the major virtues of J.I.P.3.

There is no doubt that compost bought from a reliable supplier is a good starting point for tomato growing in containers, but the cost is a point to be kept in mind. Thus, using 9-inch pots or their equivalent in volume, a bushel of compost is needed for every six plants. This puts the starting cost in regard to compost alone at 20p. to 25p. per plant.

With the weight of ripe fruit which one can reasonably expect to obtain with culture in containers under sheltered conditions, this cost would still only represent a few pence per pound, but even so one could be excused for seeking a cheaper compost until experience of the method has been gained.

The ideal from the point of view of convenience would obviously be the use of the ordinary garden soil as the starting point for the container compost. With the great majority of garden soils this, in fact, can be done successfully but success depends upon recognizing the limitations and shortcomings of such soil for use in containers, and of rectifying these faults.

Now, in the first place, an essential feature of J.I. composts is that the fibrous loam employed is first steamed to free it from harmful insects, fungus growths and bacteria, while at the same time releasing certain plant nutrients and modifying the physical structure. This cleansing of the soil has been shown by the John Innes workers to be very essential for seedling raising and for general propagation, and it has certain advantages in connection with the final potting compost even with large strong-growing plants, such as tomatoes and even where the loam is taken from meadow land which, because crops had not been grown upon it, would normally be considered sweet and clean. Obviously then, if we are going to used the heavily cultivated soil from the garden, this cleansing, or partial sterilization to use the technical term, is all the more important.

Fortunately, this is not beyond the means of even the back-

33

yard gardener and special apparatus, though making the job easier, is not essential.

First of all, however, the soil itself. This should be taken from an area which has grown satisfactory flowers or vegetables but which has not been dressed with manure, fertilizers or lime for some months at least. The best plan, I find, is to skim off the top 1½–2 inches over a fairly large area rather than to dig out to a spit or so deep. The reason here is that the top soil is usually the most fertile from the all-important angle of physical condition. Also, of course, holes have to be filled in with odd shovels of soil from here and there, whereas the loss of a shallow surface layer is not missed.

All surface growth of weeds must be removed first and it is best to collect the soil when it is nicely moist in the autumn rather than soaked and sticky with winter rains. Stones should be removed and lumps broken down by passing the soil through a ½-inch mesh sieve.

The simplest method of 'cleaning' the soil involves the use of the chemical, formaldehyde, and this can be obtained readily and at modest cost in concentrated liquid form from garden shops.

We apply formaldehyde as a 2 per cent dilution of the concentrate and, in practical terms, this means almost exactly ½ pint added to 3 gallons of water. Now, this pungent chemical is not the most pleasant of materials to use as the gas given off makes the eyes run and irritates the nose. This effect is all the more obvious as the treatment is best carried out in the confined space of a shed or garage, but plenty of ventilation should be allowed; and as with most things which are not positively dangerous, one gets used to the smell! There is always the consolation, too, that formaldehyde vapour is a germicide which combats the common cold!

The warmer the soil at the time of treatment the better will be the effect. It certainly should not be in a frozen condition or the sterilizer will tend to break down and leave harmful residues which persist for weeks or even months and render the soil useless for any purpose.

The procedure is as follows: The moist, but not wet soil is spread out in a layer as nearly as possible 6 inches deep and it helps a lot if the floor is concrete with a drain nearby. The diluted formaldehyde is then sprinkled over from a rosed can, a little at a time, and the soil stirred with a fork between applications. The aim is to put 2 to 3 gallons of the mixture on to each square yard of this flat-topped, 6-inch deep heap. Very sandy soils (which are not ideal for our purpose) may not be able to hold as much fluid as this, but provided application and stirring are continued until the right amount has been used or liquid starts to leak away from the bottom of the heap, all will be well.

Clean sacks, previously damped over with the solution, or a ground sheet, should now be laid over the heap to cover it completely and a period of three or four days allowed for the solution and the gas it gives off to work.

At the end of this time our aim is to remove the remaining formaldehyde as quickly as possible and to this end the covering is removed and the heap stirred with a *clean* fork every day or two for a fortnight. As the soil dries out the formaldehyde disappears, mainly as vapour into the air, and when no smell remains the soil can be used. As, however, even a trace remaining will kill plants, I like to make sure at this stage when no further smell is apparent, by putting a handful of the soil into a clean press-top container, such as a treacle tin, and standing the tin on a stove or other hot surface for a few minutes. Then, if when the lid is prised off, neither the nose nor the eyes (the latter are usually the more sensitive) detect formaldehyde vapour, all is in order.

The soil, now cleansed of harmful pests and diseases, should be transferred with a *clean* shovel to a box such as a sugar crate or to a barrel previously scrubbed out with the formaldehyde solution and allowed to dry. If this is not possible, sacks previously soaked in the solution and dried can be employed, but on no account should the clean soil be left lying round or given any chance to be re-contaminated by pest or disease.

Formaldehyde used in this way does a good job, but hard-coated seeds can resist the solution and survive. For this reason some gardeners prefer to skim off the top 2 inches or so of soil—which contain most of the recently deposited weed seeds—and to use the only slightly less fertile second 2-inch layer.

The other methods of soil cleansing involve raising the temperature to the point where all insect life, most weed seeds, harmful fungi, the undesirable bacteria and other micro-organisms are killed, but stopping short of the complete sterilization which would render the soil an inert, lifeless mass. In effect, then, heat treatment involves controlled 'partial-sterilization', and this term is widely used in connection with all soil-cleansing work though it is frequently shortened to 'sterilization'.

In commercial practice the soil temperature is raised to close on 212° F. (boiling point) by introducing steam from a boiler by means of perforated grids. This is not within our means in the garden and we need something involving less apparatus and more in keeping with the small quantities of soil concerned.

The easiest way, now that electricity is available almost everywhere, is to use an electric sterilizer. Supply details of this apparatus are given in the Appendix, and the gardener who is not unduly concerned with expense will find it a ready solution to his soil-cleansing problems.

The principle involved in one type of electric sterilizer is interesting. The insulated inner soil-box has the long sides made of metal and the short sides and bottom of non-conduct-ing material. The metal sides of the box are connected to the mains supply and, normally, with no solid medium between the sides, no current will pass. If, however, before switching on the current, *moist* soil is packed firmly into the box, a current is able to pass and the intensity of the current will depend upon the moisture content and tightness of the soil. Very wet soil offers too little resistance and the current is so great that the fuses will be blown. Dry soil, on the other hand, is a fairly good insulator and the current passing would be slight. The requirement is sufficient moisture to conduct the current freely but with sufficient resistance from the soil to cause heat to be generated. The soil then acts in a similar manner to the element of an electric fire but, as the temperature rises, the water in the soil turns into steam, escapes from the box and the soil gradually dries out.

These sterilizers are fitted with a current meter and when the reading falls to a given figure, sterilization is complete. The mains supply is then switched off and the soil turned out in a thin layer to cool.

From my experience, electric sterilizing is both convenient and effective, and the only factors requiring experience are the original moisture content of the soil and the degree of compression in the box. I find that, with my rather light soil, a moisture content slightly greater than the ideal potting condition is satisfactory providing the soil is pressed down firmly with the fingers. It is essential to press the soil well against the metal sides and if, when the current is switched on, the dial reading is below the given starting figure—which means very slow heating—I find that the trouble can be overcome by switching off, removing the cover and pouring a little water along the soil surface immediately against the plates. This allows the current to 'get started' and the job can be carried out according to instructions.

This method is excellent, but it does involve the purchase of the sterilizer and a certain expenditure for electricity. I have personally 'baked' soil in the garden on numerous occasions with equally satisfactory results, but careful management is required and the following details will be of interest to the 'no-apparatus' gardener.

The baking of soil involves nothing more than heating it under controlled conditions on a metal plate. My own procedure is as follows:

All 'garden wood' obtained from pruning or lopping fruit trees, reducing the height of deciduous hedges or strong-growing shrubs such as Philadelphus (Mock Orange) and even the hard stalks of herbaceous plants, is piled up in an out-of-the-way corner for the sap to dry out. Then, one dry, windy day, when no other jobs are insistent, a rough fireplace is built on the ground immediately behind a low retaining wall. The reason for this choice of site will be apparent in a moment.

For this fireplace I use concrete blocks from a war-time anti-blast wall because they are heavy and do not shift during subsequent operations. Bricks can, however, be used if due care is taken when moving the plate.

The blocks are placed in two parallel rows 18 inches apart with a narrow air-gap between each block. The fireplace is made about 3 feet long in order to give support to a sheet of old corrugated iron, 4 feet long by 2 ft. 6 in. wide.

Some of the wood is now burnt between the walls and gradually the whole length and breadth of the fireplace is a bed of red embers. In between stoking and controlling the fire, the top 2 inches or so of part of the adjacent chrysanthemum bed which is in a good fertile condition as a result of years of generous treatment, is skimmed off into a heap. Lumps are broken down and stones, etc., removed by passing the soil through a $\frac{1}{2}$ inch-mesh sieve.

At this stage the corrugated sheet is laid over the blocks and a layer of the soil is poured on from a bucket to give a depth, when smoothed over, of no more than 2 inches deep in the valleys. The soil is covered with an old sack and more fuel added to the fire. The need for this periodic refuelling is the reason for making the fireplace immediately behind the retaining wall—it saves a lot of back-bending and standing on one's head to see what is happening under the sheet! Incidentally, experience shows that around 12 inches is the best height for the walls to allow sufficient air and yet have the sheet as near as possible to the fire-bed. Also, it pays to have the sheet sloping slightly upwards towards the back to encourage the smoke to rise away from the stoking end. The alternative is a somewhat kippered condition by the time the job is completed!

With a good brisk fire the thin layer of soil is beginning to steam briskly after about 10 minutes and this will be seen even without removing the sack. At this stage the sack should be laid aside and the soil raked over to prevent the layer against the metal from drying out completely and burning to material like brick dust. This condition must be avoided at all cost since burnt soil is useless for our purpose and this is the reason for having the soil thoroughly moist at the start. If the layer against the metal is obviously burning, the heat is too intense and the soil is too dry. For the next batch go easy with the stoking and water the soil lightly through a rose.

After raking over the soil, the sack should be replaced for a further 5–10 minutes. At the completion of this total heating period of 15–20 minutes the soil should be scalding hot to the hand and in a still moist but friable condition. It is now swept with a clean broom on to a clean ground sheet suitably placed, transferred to a clean concrete surface to cool rapidly in a thin layer and, when several batches have been done, stored in a clean, covered box or a sack.

The baking of soil has been criticized as a sterilizing process on the grounds that the degree and period of heating cannot be controlled accurately. From my own experience, however, if a thin layer of really moist soil is treated according to the stated routine, an acceptable and consistent result is obtained.

Soil baked in this manner and used as the loam fraction for J.I. composts has given me no trouble with germination of even delicate flower seeds nor with pricked out or potted seedlings, which indicates that it has not been overheated. On the other hand, the almost entire absence of weed germination shows that the necessary degree of cleansing has been achieved. Certainly it is a more practical method than the frequently recommended and slow job of steaming relatively tiny quantities of soil in a pail or bag suspended in a gas copper.

The quantity of soil to be sterilized must depend upon the plans worked out for the season ahead. It should be borne in mind that a bushel of J.I. compost will be required for every six 9-inch pots and that roughly half by volume of this compost is soil. On the basis of a bushel of moist soil weighing about 1 cwt. for the average suburban gardener who has a small greenhouse and who intends to grow a dozen or so tomatoes outdoors with a like number to follow on the seed-raising season in the house, 2 cwt. of sterilized soil will be a minimum requirement and 3 cwt. will be a wise provision.

Having settled the major problem of a supply of 'clean' soil, the rest of the job of making up a suitable compost for the containers follows on quite simply. As I have pointed out, the J.I. composts have so many points in their favour that it is foolish to depart from the established formulae. The high-grade brown spongy peat required is readily obtainable at garden shops and, considering its virtues, is not expensive.

Then there is the question of sand. Using the wrong grade of sand is, I think, the gardener's commonest mistake when making up soil mixtures whether for seed sowing or the various stages of potting. The purpose of using sand in a compost is very fully discussed in *Seed and Potting Compost* by Lawrence and Newell and, in fact, this book covers the whole subject of

The Container Compost

composts so thoroughly that I need only emphasize the points which are often passed over in practice as being unimportant.

Sand, unlike soil or coarse organic matter such as peat, is required for no purpose other than that of 'opening up' the compost. A fine, silty soil soon becomes compact and poorly aerated when it is watered and relatively large particles must be added to prevent this condition. Obviously, then, adding a fine, sticky sand such as the type used by builders will do little good and may even make matters worse. Within reason, the coarser the sand we use the better and, if J.I. grade sand is not obtainable, the $\frac{1}{4}$-inch siftings of washed gravel can be made to serve.

So much for the physical ingredients of the container compost—the part of the compost mainly concerned with encouraging and maintaining strong roots. Now comes the question of food reserves. Obviously it is no use having roots unless there is an ample supply of nutrients for them to absorb. Admittedly we could use a compost in the containers which was very poor in plant foods and rely upon feeding during the growing season. Generally, however, it is better to start off with a fair reserve of food and look upon growing-season feeding as merely supplementing the original supplies.

For this reason J.I. composts include fertilizers and, for pot work, J.I. Base has been worked out to give the right balance of nitrogen, phosphates and potash for normal growth of a wide range of plants. It will be noted from the J.I. compost details given in the Appendix that chalk (carbonate of lime) is added as well as J.I. Base. If the garden soil used in the compost is normally well limed the addition of chalk to the compost is not required as tomatoes prefer slightly acid soil conditions. I find from experience that, starting with soil that shows a positive test for lime, it is better to avoid adding further lime to the compost and to rely upon occasional 'feeds' with carbonate of lime during the growing season to counteract the acidifying effects of the soluble-solid or liquid feeds which are, deservedly,

41

becoming so popular for tomatoes, chrysanthemums and other intensively grown crops.

This test for 'reserve' lime in the soil is a simple one which anyone can carry out and interpret correctly and which is practical and reliable. A teaspoonful of the soil in question, with any obvious lumps of chalk removed, is put into a cup or glass and is just wetted—not flooded—with vinegar or the acid from an old accumulator. If there is any sign of frothing or bubbling, plenty of free lime is present and, certainly for tomatoes, no more is needed. If the application of the acid solution has no visible effect, it is as well to add the carbonate of lime required by the J.I. formula plus a further 2 oz. per bushel.

With all the ingredients to hand there is nothing complicated about making up J.I.P.3—the degree of richness of the J.I. Potting Compost which we need for use in the containers. As with all other jobs, however, experience points the way to easier working and avoidance of mistakes and the following points are worth noting.

The garden soil—our version of the 'loam' required by the J.I. formula—the peat and the sand are all in 'clean' condition. Obviously, then, they should be mixed on a clean surface and previously washed-down concrete is ideal.

The soil will still be moist and the sand or fine gravel is either moist as bought or, at least, takes water easily. Not so the peat, however. Good quality peat is dust-dry in the bags or bales, and peat which feels moist to the touch should be avoided at the time of purchase—especially if one is buying by weight rather than volume. After all, volume for volume, peat is very light compared with water and there is no point in buying water at the price of peat!

It pays handsomely, then, to insist on really dry peat but, when preparing to make up the J.I. compost, we must allow for the fact that dry peat repels water and is none too easy to moisten. Moist it must be, however, before it is measured and mixed in

The Container Compost

with the sand and soil and this is the easiest and best way of doing the job. Turn out a bag of peat or break up part of a bale on to the concrete surface and sprinkle with water from a rosed can. Turn the layer of peat with a clean shovel or spade and sprinkle again. Carry on with this process until the original light colour of the peat has darkened to chestnut and a handful oozes water when squeezed. This may take ten minutes or longer, but it is time very well spent since peat mixed in dry condition may remain virtually dry in the compost for a long period and cause trouble. When the peat appears well saturated, pile it into a heap for surplus water to drain away, since sloppy-wet material is difficult to handle.

Measure everything as accurately as possible using a 2-gallon bucket for the physical ingredients and a pair of scales or a scaled measure for lime and fertilizers.

Remember that the physical ingredients—the loam, peat and sand—are all quoted by volume in the formula and that, particularly with the moist peat, it should be loose volume. In other words, don't press the peat down into the bucket.

Refer to the Appendix for practical notes on mixing, etc., and—*keep strictly to the formula!*

SOILLESS COMPOSTS

While the John Innes Composts are still widely used and, when correctly prepared, are unsurpassed for reliability and ease of management, soilless composts are rapidly gaining favour with both amateur and commercial growers.

This type of compost is based upon physical ingredients which are readily obtainable and stored in standard form, such as sphagnum peat and fine sand. Since they do not involve soil in any form, the variation in results which can arise with J.I. composts is avoided and if the same technique of management is employed on all occasions, the results are reliably uniform.

43

The Container Compost

It should be noted, however, that the watering procedure with these composts based largely or entirely upon peat differs from that to which we have become accustomed with soil-based composts. We have to some extent to 're-learn' our methods of growing where soilless composts are used either for propagating or in containers or rings.

Most soilless composts are based upon the work carried out at the University of California which led to the well-known 'UC' composts. Typical of this type is 'EFF' Compost which is widely available through retail sources but this is only one of numerous proprietary brands. Of somewhat different concept is Fison's 'Levington' compost. This is based solely on selected grades of peat as physical ingredient and has the virtue of being very light in weight compared with soilless composts involving sand as well as peat.

I have used these various soilless composts myself parallel to J.I. composts with equal success once the different management technique has been mastered and I can recommend them as a modern development which achieves uniformity of results with elimination of the variable and sometimes adverse factors associated with soil.

Chapter 4

OBTAINING THE PLANTS

Having selected the site and, where necessary, erected suitable shelter from the cold quarters, prepared the border soil for rooting through or decided upon ring culture or straw-bale culture, thoughts must be turned to the all-important question of the source of the plants which will be needed in the latter half of April.

Now, this is anything up to a month earlier than tomato plants normally appear, along with the more tender bedding subjects, on display stands outside garden shops. Under the normal circumstances of culture in the open garden, late May planting is quite early enough for any degree of safety in the average spring, but we need an earlier batch and, incidentally, better grown plants than the poor, shivering specimens so commonly offered at around sixpence each.

There are several ways of solving this problem. The first involves making arrangements in good time—no later than the end of February—either direct with a local nurseryman or through the local garden shop. Nurseries usually raise several batches of tomato plants; the first in January–February for growing on in heated greenhouses, the second for cold house work in March–April, and the third for the outdoor trade.

Plants from the last of the cold house supplies will suit our purpose as far as time is concerned, and they will have been fairly well 'hardened' off under cool conditions. It is as well, however, to look upon such plants as still fairly tender and to continue the 'toughening-up' process for a few days before setting them out in the containers. Some points on this subject will be found detailed below in connection with propagation.

Such plants should be requested for mid-April, and it is best if they are in large 60 (3½ inch) clay pots. Well grown and hardened plants are worth 7p. to 10p. each and are a much better proposition than plants from boxes a month later at a third of the price. After all, it takes only 1 lb. tomatoes per plant to cover this apparently high initial cost! I have, personally, also done well with soil-block plants and, although watering during the final hardening-off period is a little more tricky, the extra compost in the standard block, over and above that contained in a 60 clay, makes for stronger establishment. Furthermore, a root-bound condition cannot occur in a soil block and this helps a great deal with the early watering when the plants are transferred to the containers. Avoid, however, taking the plants in the 'paper' pots, into which they are often transferred for transport. The sudden change to non-porous conditions can seriously harm the health of the roots unless transfer to the containers is to take place within a matter of hours. I am purposely making an issue of this point since the essential for an early crop is quick establishment of the plants and an early check to the roots is never completely overcome.

To summarize on this source of supply: make definite arrangements about the time when the plants are required; specify that they should be in clay pots or soil blocks, and at least partly hardened-off; try to arrange that the variety is one known to do well out of doors (see Chapter 9), and don't be put off by undoubtedly well-meaning advice to wait until the end of May!

Another way of getting the plants at the right time is to make arrangements with a friend who has a greenhouse which he heats sufficiently in the late winter and early spring to raise half-hardy annuals and, probably, his own tomatoes for planting in the house. It is certainly a cheaper way since one can always recompense his trouble by making some other gardening contribution.

Then, for those who have even quite modest facilities, there is the obvious method of raising one's own plants from seed. There is for me, and I think for most gardeners, much more satisfaction in growing a crop right from the beginning than by acquiring the plants when all the interesting early development has been completed.

It must be borne in mind, however, that if home-raised plants are to compare as regards stage of development with those bought at planting time, the seed will need to be sown during the first weeks of the new year and that, in consequence, it must be possible to maintain a brisk growing temperature no matter how cold the weather.

Some gardeners are willing to maintain the required minimum temperature of 55° F. in the whole greenhouse throughout the cold months of the year, because various pot plants are being grown for home decoration. Most of us, however, find this far too expensive in terms of fuel, especially if only propagation is involved and I feel it may be useful to describe the method of raising tomatoes which I have used successfully and economically for some years.

Starting at the beginning, the greenhouse is completely cleared when the last chrysanthemum blooms have been cut around the Christmas period. The whole superstructure, including the glass, is thoroughly scrubbed down with a tar distillate disinfectant solution. The bench slats and supports are likewise thoroughly cleansed before being returned to the house. Full ventilation is given for a few days to disperse the sterilizer fumes, and the house is now ready for the start of the propagating season around mid-January.

If repainting of the house is scheduled or any repairs

are necessary, this is a suitable time to carry out these jobs.

The kingpin of the whole job, an electrically heated propagating case, is now assembled on the bench. These propagators can be bought ready to use in various sizes, but even small ones are somewhat expensive, and it is worth while to make one of light timber.

My own propagator consists of a lower lid-less box of external dimensions 26½ in. by 24½ in. by 6 in. deep, and provided with a ledge an inch wide just below the top. A crossbeam is fitted with two electric light sockets which are wired to an external plug.

Another box of dimensions 25 in. by 23 in. by 8 in. deep, stands on the ledge but, in this instance, the bottom consists of a thin zinc sheet nailed to fit closely. The top box also has a ledge just below the top to allow a cloche to be accommodated when required, the end sheets of glass being held by vertical wires which push into holes drilled in the short-side timbers.

To operate the case, ordinary electric light bulbs of selected capacity are inserted in the sockets, 2 inches of thoroughly wet sphagnum peat is placed over the metal sheet of the top box, and this box is stood on the ledge of the lower one.

Until such time as the greater head room provided by a cloche is required, the top box is covered with glass laid flat. Two equal sheets are desirable, as a variable central gap for ventilation can then be obtained by sliding the sheets apart.

The propagating case is installed on the greenhouse bench to bring it as much up into the light as possible. The seed of the chosen variety is now sown, using J.I.P.1 compost, in a receptacle of size appropriate to the number of plants one requires.

Bearing in mind that the seedlings will be a week or ten days old at the most when pricked-out, there need be no fear of overcrowding from fairly thick sowing, and to sow 200 or 300 seeds in a standard seed-tray when the requirements of early plants is no more than a dozen or so is obviously wasteful.

Obtaining the Plants

Under such circumstances, a shallow earthenware seed-pan or, failing this, a 5-inch pot reduced in capacity by crocking to within 3 inches of the top, is more in keeping with requirements.

Roughly twice as many seeds as the number of plants ultimately required are scattered evenly over the surface of the well-firmed and levelled compost, and a $\frac{1}{4}$ inch covering of finely sifted compost is given. Thorough saturation of the compost without disturbance of the seeds is ensured by standing the pan or pot in a pail containing sufficient water to reach nearly to the compost surface. Water is drawn up by suction and, when tiny beads of moisture glisten on the surface, saturation is complete.

After allowing surplus water to drain away, the seed-pan is placed on the moistened peat bed in the propagator. The top glass is put into position and the heat switched on.

Other pans or boxes of seeds or cuttings can be accommodated at the same time, provided it is borne in mind that within three weeks a good deal of space will be required for the young plants pricked-out into 3-inch pots, and other subjects will need to be accommodated elsewhere.

Ordinary household electric bulbs certainly provide the most convenient source of heat, and I find that, with the greenhouse air temperature down to freezing point a good deal of the time, about 50 watts in bulb capacity is required to maintain around 60° F. air temperature in a propagator of this size.

To avoid overheating in one spot, it is best to wire the lower heating compartment to accommodate two 25 watt bulbs in roughly diagonal position. Ordinary household bulbs placed on their sides rather than in the usual hanging position have a considerably reduced life, but they are not unduly expensive to replace and the special heavy-duty bulbs intended for horizontal fixing are too dear to be justified.

49

Obtaining the Plants

By using bulbs of different power and sliding the top glass to give more or less ventilation, it is surprisingly easy to maintain a fairly steady temperature.

The peat is kept moist by a heavy damping every day or two, and by the seventh day the seedlings usually appear.

Investigations at the John Innes Institution have shown some advantage in pricking-out the seedlings as soon as the little seed leaves have expanded—about three days after germination —but for ease of handling, I prefer to leave them another week, and I find the result entirely satisfactory.

Previously washed and dried 3-inch pots are required for pricking-out, and J.I.P.1 compost is again used. With this sharply drained compost, no crocking of the pots is necessary, and the job is very simply carried out, but it certainly needs a delicate touch to avoid damage to the tiny plants.

The roots are gently loosened from the compost of the pan by means of a wooden label and individual seedlings are separated by gently holding the seed leaves—never the stems— and disengaging the roots.

The correct way to pot is to have the 60's half full of compost which has been lightly firmed by rapping the pot, to hold the seedling by a seed leaf with the roots touching the compost, and to fill in further compost so that the final level, after gentle firming, is about $\frac{3}{8}$ inch below the rim and with the seed leaves close to or touching the surface of the compost.

The final stage is to give the batch of pricked-off plants a gentle drench through a fine rose and to stand them back pot-thick in the propagator.

The same temperature conditions will apply and no ventilation is needed for the first week unless, due to the greenhouse itself being heated by the sun, the top glass of the propagator has to be slid back an inch or two to keep the temperature from rising above 70° F.

For the first ten days or so, the young plants benefit by the high humidity arising from restricted ventilation, but gradually more air is allowed by night as well as day consistent with the temperature falling no lower than 55° F. The greenhouse itself, during this early propagation period, remains closed unless the weather is exceptionally warm.

Every morning and evening the glass is turned over to disperse the beads of moisture which condense upon it and, every few days, water evaporated from the peat, by the heat beneath, is replaced by heavy sprinkling.

Though with the sharply drained J.I. compost it is impossible to cause waterlogging of the pots, I find it best to be rather sparing with water as the bed of moist peat from which water is continually being evaporated maintains a humid atmosphere and the compost does not dry out rapidly.

It must also be borne in mind that the intensity of light is none too good under average winter conditions and that, in consequence, growth must be restricted somewhat or the plants will become tall, spindly and pale in colour. At this stage I usually water every third or fourth day, giving a ¼ pint or slightly less to each plant.

As the plants grow bigger and the occasional sunny day necessitates ventilation of the case to keep the temperature within bounds, more water will be required and one has to be guided by the appearance of the compost and the condition of the plants.

By the middle of March, my mid-January sown plants have developed two or three true leaves and the foliage is just beginning to touch. If the plants were left pot-thick, they would soon become drawn and weak so more generous spacing has to be arranged. Although by now I have commenced to heat the actual greenhouse for general propagation, I find it is rather too sudden a change to transfer the little plants straight from the cosy conditions of the propagator to the drier air and more changeable temperature of the open bench. I prefer to space them out in the case and to remove the glass entirely during the daytime.

After a few days the glass is left off at night as well, and then the transfer to the greenhouse bench or shelf can proceed without check to growth.

The proof of how well or badly the plants have been grown up to this stage is given by the condition of the seed leaves. If they are still firm and green, growth has been steady and unchecked; a shrivelled condition, though not indicating that the plants are useless, does nevertheless mean that there is room for improvement in the growing technique.

Now, at the end of March with the weather improving and plenty of light, growing presents no real problems, though one must be prepared for the occasional loss of a plant from damping-off. If more than the odd plant goes down in this way, it is as well to water them all with Cheshunt Compound solution as described in Chapter 8.

It should be borne in mind also that a starved, pot-bound condition must be avoided and, to this end, I usually pot-on into 48's (5-inch pots) using J.I.P.2 compost to keep the plants growing strongly until it is convenient to plant up in the final 9-inch pots or in the border of the greenhouse.

Watering, ventilation, overhead damping in sunny weather, and control of pests all follow the normal routine for the glasshouse and, in fact, after the early raising period, the tomato is by no means a fussy subject.

Plants raised from January sowing and brought along as indicated will be those required for growing in the greenhouse itself during the summer months. They are too early for outdoor culture unless the bench space available allows of a batch being planted in containers and gradually hardened off for transfer to the outdoor growing quarters as well-developed plants with the first truss in flower towards the end of April.

This production of well-developed plants for outdoor growing is ideal from the point of view of earliness, but where green-house space in the spring is likely to be limited, it is better to sow a further batch of seed of a suitable outdoor variety around mid-February and to bring these later plants along in the propagator parallel to the earlier batch required for growing on in the greenhouse.

From the point of view of a heavy crop as apart from the maximum earliness it is always better to set out a small well-hardened plant than one which has been held back under glass and is setting fruit. The latter are usually unduly restricted by the bottom fruit and fail to 'get away' freely.

So much for my own way of propagation, and there now remains a brief record of methods which friends have adopted with a fair measure of success.

Where the greenhouse is not wired for electric heating a propagating case can still be used provided the lower box is made rather deeper to accommodate a small oil lamp and a trap door is contrived to allow the lamp to be withdrawn for clean-ing and filling as required. In this instance, the heat tends to be concentrated mainly in one spot, but the bed of moist peat in the upper compartment helps to smooth out this effect and the results are fairly uniform. The only real difficulty is that with the greenhouse itself unheated, it will not be possible to space out the plants on the bench until they are approaching the final potting stage and require to be hardened off. This means one must not attempt to raise more than the propagator case can hold at the 4-inch square spacing which is the minimum for later development. This amounts to about two dozen plants in a propagator of the size described.

Then there was the circumstance of the gardener with no glass other than a cold frame. This would seem a hopeless proposition for raising even moderately early plants, but if the floor is excavated to sufficient depth to accommodate the propagator and, in due course, a superimposed low-barn cloche beneath the frame light, the method is quite practicable.

It is important, however, to give the plants all possible light and they should be brought as close to the frame light as possible.

Still another way is to turn the cold frame into a miniature heated greenhouse. I have seen excellent plants of various types, including really early tomatoes, raised by this means and the details are as follows:

A brick-built structure is most suitable as frames with walls of thin wood or asbestos sheet tend to lose heat too rapidly. These types can, however, be rendered much more retentive of heat by applying an internal lining of the bituminized glass-wool sheeting now widely used for domestic insulation purposes.

The first step is to remove roughly 6 inches of the earth floor of the frame and replace with clean, sharp sand or with well-washed cinder or breeze. A 4-inch layer is first put down, levelled and well-firmed and then a mains voltage soil-heating cable is laid in zigzag formation to provide between 6 and 10 watts per square foot of floor area. Thus, a cable rated at 100 watts (consumption 1/10th unit per hour) would be sufficient for heating an area of between 10 and 16 square feet.

These modern cables are very safe if correctly installed but, if preferred, a transformer unit supplying low voltage current to bare wires can be employed with equal effect. Here, the wires are cheap to replace, but the transformer involves a fairly high initial cost. With either method, it is a requirement of local electricity authorities that the actual connection to the mains supply shall be by a qualified electrician.

With the wires laid, the remaining 2 inches of cinder or sand is filled in and firmed to a level surface.

When operating both day and night, the wires provide sufficient heat to keep boxes of seedlings or pots and the air itself reasonably warm in all but the hardest weather. A thick covering with sacks is desirable at night and it is a useful addition to have a further cable or wires running round the sides just above floor level to provide direct air heating. In this way, a growing temperature can be maintained even when there are several degrees of frost outside. Such heating wires are, of course, installed after applying any additional insulation which may be necessary to the walls of the frame.

A frame adapted in this manner is capable of raising sturdy plants at the time required, but ventilation—always the most difficult problem with small heated structures—requires both skill and experience to ensure that there shall be sufficient air circulation without undue loss of heat.

The only other method of frame heating which I have found satisfactory is a hot-bed constructed to give mild heat over a long period. This source of heat is, however, out of the question for most of us to-day due to the shortage and high cost of fresh stable manure.

Finally, there is the circumstance of no glass of any sort but a desire nevertheless to raise tomatoes and other seedlings. Here again, the propagating case comes into the picture and a window of a room of southern aspect takes the place of the greenhouse. The propagator is stood on a table as close to the window as possible, and exactly the same procedure of propagation is followed as previously described.

The illustrations show a propagator in operation under these conditions.

When following this method, however, it should be borne in mind that even in a bay window most of the light reaches the plants from an oblique angle and that, in consequence, they will tend to bend towards the window. This tendency must be overcome and, short of having the propagator on some form of turntable, the only way is to turn the seed-pan or each pot through a half circle each day. Admittedly, the plants have a busy time turning from side to side, but they nevertheless make quite a creditable show!

Obtaining the Plants

Under these circumstances it is unwise to sow the seed before the end of February as the light would be too limiting in the early year.

We have, then, several ways of raising the plants effectively and this brief outline should be sufficient to give the enthusiast the essentials which can be applied or adapted as required.

It is as well to bear in mind as a general principle of propagation that the earlier the sowing, the less sturdy will be the plants. This is due to there being insufficient intensity and duration of daylight in the depth of winter for ideal growth. The commercial grower surmounts this deficiency to a degree by irradiating the seedlings and young plants by means of high power mercury vapour (HPMV) lamps, but these are too expensive to install for average amateur conditions. Some improvement in winter growth can, however, be achieved by the use of modern fluorescent tube lights suspended 12 to 24 in. above the plants.

Even better is the mercury fluorescent lamp produced by Simplex of Cambridge Ltd of Sawston, Cambridge, specified as MBFT/V 160 watt and costing about £6.25p. complete with fittings, with replacement lamps at £3.95p. These are obtainable on order from local electricity board showrooms and advice on the safe installation of electric power under the humid conditions of the greenhouse is readily available from this Authority.

By our own efforts in raising we may produce something a good deal less than perfect specimens, the seed leaves may look a trifle weary by the time the plants are due for the final pots and the growth may be taller in relation to spread of the foliage than we should like to see but, given well-prepared compost and an intelligent application of the simple principles of growing, the results will thoroughly justify the effort.

Chapter 5

TOMATOES IN THE GREENHOUSE

M

any gardeners seem to look upon greenhouse culture as something fundamentally different from growing out of doors. Their use of glass protection stops short at the end of the propagating season, and from then on the greenhouse serves little purpose other than to accommodate a few pot plants and as a depository for seed-trays, compost and the hundred and one odds and ends of gardening equipment.

This is a pity, because there should be few weeks in the year when the greenhouse is not being used for growing a worthwhile crop.

It may be that highly specialized knowledge is thought to be required to grow a crop under glass, and then there are the questions of heating, ventilation, watering and feeding which, perhaps not unreasonably, tend to add up in prospect to something beyond the capabilities and purse of the home gardener.

In fact, however, growing under glass is nothing more than a logical extension of the protected conditions which we have sought to contrive for growing tomatoes out of doors. A greenhouse is merely a structure which gives a greater measure of protection against the elements than anything which can be achieved out of doors and, if we look upon it in that way, there need be nothing at all unusual about growing a crop under glass.

The tomato is an obvious choice for growing in the greenhouse in the late spring and summer months because it is naturally a warm-climate plant and flourishes with the protection which a greenhouse can provide. Furthermore, because it grows happily enough out of doors during warm periods, it does not need much artificial heat in the early season to thrive when given the extra protection of the surrounding glass.

Indeed, as I pointed out in the Foreword of this book, the tomato fits in very nicely between the period when the greenhouse is fully occupied with seedlings and cuttings and when it is required for housing the Late-flowering chrysanthemums. Whereas out of doors one is doing quite well to ripen 4 or 5 lb. of fruit per plant and with much of this going well on into the autumn, the same plants, given reasonable attention in the greenhouse, may well give twice this quantity and with ripening commencing several weeks earlier. This would entail planting towards the end of March with heating for but a few weeks and then only between sunset and sunrise, except during unusually cold spells.

For the average small greenhouse, this involves only the most simple of heating equipment and a few shillings spent in oil or electricity will bring the plants along in that steady condition of growth which promotes, if not a very early crop, certainly a heavy one.

Let us see, then, how we can use the greenhouse to provide tomatoes before the outdoor crop commences to ripen even under the most favourable conditions and in the best of summers.

In the first place, there is, from my experience, every advantage to be gained by planning to grow in containers. Container culture is so much more flexible than growing in the soil of the greenhouse, because the young plants can be transferred to the containers at the ideal stage of development and, instead of having to clear the house and the propagating bench, the containers can be accommodated for a week or two on the bench itself and other plants being raised from seed or cuttings can remain in the house, thus using the heated space to best advantage.

The plants, whether bought in or raised as described in Chapter 4, will by now, early in April, have reached the stage of at least showing the first truss in the head. Well-grown plants will be about 9 inches high, the spread of leaves will be something of the same order and the seed leaves or cotyledons will still be firm and green. Another sign of a vigorous yet sturdy and well-balanced condition is a heavy growth of hairs on the stem, leaf stalks and, to a less marked degree, on the individual leaves themselves. This gives almost a halo effect when the plants are standing against the early morning sun striking through the greenhouse, and is a sure sign that all is well.

Plants still in the 3-inch pots will be approaching a root-bound condition and there should be a clean white sheath of active root encircling the ball from top to bottom. Such heavy rooting in a limited space means that the plant is actively searching for more food and water and will very soon be showing signs of starvation if a further supply is not provided. It is the critical stage when even a few days of neglect can cause a stunting and premature truss development which is difficult to correct thereafter.

This is the reason why I invariably pot on into 48's as soon as the roots in the 60's are working strongly round the ball of soil. Growth then continues in a balanced condition, and the development of the first truss at the expense of extension growth is prevented.

Often, however, plants bought in will be in more or less root-bound condition and it is wise to go through the intermediate 48 potting stage to bring the roots gradually out into the new compost.

Prior to potting, thorough moistening of the 60 ball should be ensured by several light waterings or, better still, by immersing the pot for 10 minutes or so in water. When the surplus water has drained, the plant having been stood back on the bench, a feed of a tomato liquid fertilizer at normal dilution should be given to ensure that the roots are supplied with sufficient nutrients to carry the growth until the new compost takes effect.

For the first few days, light watering each day close to the stem will be needed to keep the mass of roots moist but, by the end of the week, the roots will be out in the new compost and watering can then be carried out normally.

This extra potting might appear to be a waste of time, but with plants pot-bound in the 60's it is by far the best way of preventing a serious check to growth.

As soon as the root system is well established in the 48's, the final potting into containers should be undertaken. In the meantime, steady growth has been maintained by free ventilation in the daytime whenever the weather allows, by damping overhead on sunny days to preserve a moist, buoyant atmosphere, and by closing the house in the late afternoon to conserve sun-heat and to allow 50–55° F. to be maintained with the minimum of artificial heat. It is surprising how careful use of the ventilators can keep down fuel costs and, at the same time, preserve the essential sturdy growth.

If the plants are to be grown by ring culture or on straw bales, bottomless containers will be used. This presents no problem if the house can be cleared of staging and the containers or 'rings' can be filled with compost direct on to the previously prepared aggregate or straw bed, but, if a further period on the bench is dictated by the needs of other plants not yet ready to go outside, an improvisation is needed.

I am usually faced with this problem myself, and I find the easiest thing to do is to stand the bottomless containers—9-inch bituminized composition pots in my case—on pieces of old asbestos tile. They can then be filled with compost, planted up, and tile and all stood back on the bench. Then, as soon as circumstances allow, the 'rings' can be carefully slid off the tiles on to the aggregate and, with care, there need be no disturbance of compost or damage to the plants.

The actual job of this final potting is no different in essentials from the potting-on from the 60's to the 48's. Whereas, however, one normally employs some of the left-over J.I.P.1 for the 48 transfer, the final potting needs a mixing of J.I.P.3.

It is well to bear in mind when preparing this batch of compost that a bushel will be needed for every five to six finals, so enough should be made to avoid the annoyance of having to leave off the potting to mix up some more.

The details of potting have been given in the chapter on Outdoor Culture, and I would merely emphasize that the compost should be thoroughly firmed especially round the sides without actual ramming, and that the ball of soil should lie just below the level of the surface of the new compost which, in turn, lies about $1\frac{1}{2}$ inches below the top of the container.

Where, incidentally, the plants are not at all pot-bound when bought-in and circumstances of greenhouse space allow the final potting in the containers to take place, the 48 stage can be omitted and the turned-out 60's planted straight in the containers. Actually, in my experience, the plants eventually are quite as good by this method, though obviously, being younger, they will not come into bearing so early under equivalent conditions of culture.

From early April onwards the plants can, if necessary, be grown without any artificial heat and, by reason of the continuous protection afforded, cropping commences some weeks earlier than in even the most sheltered outdoor situations. The cropping, too, carries on for a longer period since the autumn frosts which put paid to the outdoor crop are excluded by the glass and the reserve of sun warmth within.

Providing the best use of natural heat is made by closing

down before the sun leaves the glass and restricting ventilation on dull days, the temperature can usually be kept above 40° F. even at night, and the plants make slow but steady progress.

Excellent tomato crops can be grown without heat and no cold house should be left empty during the summer months.

Without doubt, however, the cost of keeping the night temperature 10 to 15 degrees above that prevailing outside is handsomely repaid in earliness of fruiting. I refer specifically to the night temperature since, in my experience, heating during the daytime from April onwards cannot be justified in a small greenhouse.

In an 8 ft. 6 in. by 6 ft. 6 in. metal-frame house I use a 500 watt ($\frac{1}{2}$ unit per hour) electric heater only between sunset and 9 a.m. during the period from planting until the end of May. The cost is about 70p. to 80p. per week and, with early April planting, the total around £7. By comparison with an unheated house alongside, I much more than regain this expenditure in the weight of fruit picked at a worth-while part of the season.

For most of us it merely means continuing heating for a few weeks beyond the propagating period while for those gardeners who are debating the purchase of a heater it is a further good reason for incurring the quite modest expense which opens up a whole new field of out-of-season growing.

Ventilation of a small house is always something of a problem. The volume is small compared with the surface area and the temperature therefore tends to fluctuate rapidly according to the weather. Allowing more or less air to enter is an obvious way of minimizing these violent changes in temperature but, apart from those who are retired from business and who can follow the moods of the weather, there is little one can do but 'open up' on sunny mornings before leaving for work or on dull, chilly days to leave it to those at home to do the necessary if the sun beats the clouds.

The ideal small house has large vents both sides in the walls

Tomatoes in the Greenhouse

and roof, but one can do quite well with roof vents only. Two are certainly better than one since off-wind ventilation is then possible and the atmosphere of the house can be kept buoyant without chilly draughts.

The practice of ventilating a greenhouse is something which can be learnt only by experience, but the basic principle is that of giving the maximum circulation of air without causing undue lowering of the temperature or incurring those drizzling draughts which plants dislike as much as we do ourselves. Most newcomers to greenhouse culture under-ventilate and, by promoting an unduly hot, stagnant atmosphere, encourage drawn, pale growth and widely spaced, weak trusses.

These comments refer to daytime ventilation; night air is desirable only in really warm weather—which means seldom before mid-June.

Watering

The watering technique for plants being grown in containers has been discussed in some detail in connection with outdoor culture and there is nothing different for plants under glass except that, with the higher temperatures prevailing, the demand for water is greater and the early ball-waterings to sustain the roots until they work out into the bulk of compost are even more vital.

With plants in containers there is no point in saturating all the compost right from the start, since to do so would be to encourage rank, leafy growth and the plants might as well have the unrestricted root-run of the greenhouse border soil.

On the other hand, to allow the ball of roots turned out from the 60- or 48-sized pot to become dry is to invite poor development of at least the first truss. Furthermore, the condition known as 'dry set' is likely to arise in which fertilization does not take place in anything like a regular manner and only a

63

few fruits are produced, usually towards the far end of the truss.

It pays to undertake this early watering very carefully and, for the first fortnight or three weeks after planting, a general watering to the point of saturating the container compost should be avoided.

As soon as most of the fruits on the bottom truss have set and the earliest are reaching the size of a large cherry, it is safe to replace ball watering by general application, and by late April or early May the plants will be needing at least a quart of water each three times a week.

This applies whether the containers are standing upon the prepared border soil, ring culture aggregate or upon straw since the influence of the underlying medium is not felt until the roots penetrate down from the container soil.

Soon, however, it will be found that the root system has extended beyond the container and is penetrating into the border soil, aggregate or straw which is in a moist condition as a result of overhead damping of the plants. From then on the roots in the container become less and less vital to the plants and, though it is desirable to apply sufficient water to the containers throughout the season to keep the compost moist, the plant draws most of its water from beneath.

Quite often, as the season advances and the plant matures, the soil in the container may be well on the dry side but the foliage does not wilt in hot sunlight. There the moisture in the border soil or ring culture aggregate is supporting the plant and we see in this example the real purpose of the container: to control growth at the early stages and to supply food and water until the root system extends beneath.

As will be seen from Chapter 6, this is only partly true of ring culture since throughout the season feeding is restricted to the container soil, and the fact that the main water requirement of the plant is supplied from the aggregate means that the con-

Ware Cross on straw bales isolated from the floor by polythene sheeting

The strong, clean roots produced in straw beds

Commercial crop on straw wads. Watering by low-level irrigation line

Typical magnesium deficiency

Wilt caused by Verticillium disease

Roots formed in coarse sand
aggregate

Typical ring and aggregate
(vermiculite) roots

The large fruit has set normally; the small, seedless
fruits are swelling as a result of hormone treatment

tainer roots have a lower requirement for water and need little more than that supplied in the course of liquid feeding, except in the hottest of weather.

Gradually then, watering in the container becomes less important and of the border soil, aggregate or straw more important. The watering procedure for ring culture is fully described in my companion book, but for the border soil, presuming that drainage is satisfactory, a thorough soaking at least once a week is required. This may mean the equivalent of 2 or 3 gallons of water per plant, but the only really satisfactory proof that the right amount of water is being applied to the border is to dig down with a trowel and make certain that the soil is thoroughly moist, but not waterlogged, a foot or so beneath the surface. If this test is made every fortnight during the main cropping period there is no difficulty in deciding whether more or less water should be given. With healthy plants, flagging of the young top foliage on a hot day is generally a fair indication that the soil at the deeper levels is drying out and that watering should be increased.

Incidentally, in the old days, considerable emphasis was laid upon the necessity for using rain-water rather than the mains for glasshouse plants and of having the water thoroughly warmed by standing for some hours in the greenhouse prior to use. Certainly soft rain-water at air temperature seems a kinder medium to apply to roots growing in warm soil, but work at the John Innes Institution showed no difference between rain-water at air temperature and that drawn straight from the mains. This applies, apparently, to the watering of seedlings, so we need not be too concerned with the nature of the water so long as the right amount is given at the right time!

HUMIDITY

In the comments on watering, reference was made to the

border soil, Ring Culture aggregate or straw being in moist condition due to overhead damping of the plants. It is very necessary that the air in the greenhouse be in a moist condition to allow the pollen grains to germinate and bring about fertilization.

On dull days, the moisture evaporated from the floor of the house and transpired by the plants themselves is sufficient to maintain the required humidity, but in bright, sunny weather extra moisture is needed.

To achieve this purpose, the plants should be heavily damped several times during the course of the day through a fine rose on the water-can. In addition to increasing the humidity, this sprinkling with water shakes the plants and releases the pollen grains. The effect, indeed, is much the same as that achieved by tapping the strings or stakes supporting the plants or 'dusting' the blooms with a rabbit's tail as was common practice at one time.

Overhead damping should, however, be done with some discretion, as the foliage must be dry when the vents are closed in the late afternoon or diseases such as mould and Botrytis will be encouraged.

Under conditions of persistently dull weather and particularly with plants which are growing too vigorously as a result of overwatering, setting is often as irregular as with a dry plant. Under such circumstances, it is worth while to induce an artificial 'set' by applying a 'hormone' solution to the truss concerned by means of a small sprayer provided with an upturned mist nozzle. Fruits induced to swell in this manner are seedless, but otherwise normal by the time they reach maturity.

In my experience, these fruit-setting preparations are worth using under adverse conditions, but with good culture they should certainly not be needed at the period of the year with which we are concerned.

Overhead damping during the heat of the day would be an

advantage from the point of view of setting the trusses right throughout the life of the plant, but there comes a time when the advantage so gained is more than offset by the foliage diseases which are encouraged when the growth is well advanced and the foliage is heavy.

By the end of May overhead damping should be discontinued, as the heavy foliage will retain too much of the water and may still be wet when the house has to be closed. In hot weather, however, with full ventilation and perhaps even the door open to keep the temperature within bounds, the air around the plants may become too dry for the higher trusses to set evenly.

This trouble can be overcome to a large degree by watering the path so that damp air is continually rising around the plants.

It is desirable, also, to apply a light shading of whitewash to the glass on the outside to break the direct rays of the sun. This can be done with a syringe when the ventilators are closed, or with a large brush, but the mixture should be very much on the thin side or the reduction in light intensity will be too great and the quality of growth will suffer in the direction of softness.

Heavy showers of rain remove most of the shading, but this is not entirely a disadvantage, as in dull, rainy weather all the light available is needed. For this reason I prefer ordinary whitewash which needs renewing from time to time rather than rain-proof mixtures which, once on, are there until removed by scrubbing.

The method of supporting the plants is exactly as described for outdoor culture against a protecting fence. As soon as growth is vigorous, and before there is any tendency for the plants to sag over, they must be provided with strings secured to the stem below a leaf and taken up to a wire tightly stretched between the gable ends of the house. This wiring is simple enough in a wood-frame house, but provision for wires is, in my experience, usually lacking in metal houses. With the latter, strong wooden or metal posts must be driven in securely to carry the overhead wires.

This is something of a problem, since at least 18 inches must be driven in and at the same time the posts should reach almost up to the glass of the roof slope.

I find that the easiest way to satisfy both requirements is to have each post made of $\frac{1}{4}$-inch angle iron and in two roughly equal sections which can be bolted together. One section is driven firmly into the floor of the house and the other piece then bolted on, thus avoiding the awkward job of trying to handle a tall and quite heavy post in one section.

These supports for the wires need to be strong and rigid, as the wire they carry will be supporting the total weight of perhaps six plants bearing anything up to 10 lb. of fruit, quite apart from the stem and foliage. Better by far to overdo the strength than to have the whole lot collapse at a critical period.

I like to make the lower tie beneath the leaf immediately under the first truss, as the bottom leaves will soon be removed and one wants to avoid the string slipping up the stem.

Training consists of taking the plant round the string to provide spiral support. Sometimes when growth is strong, it is none too easy to 'twist' the growth without risk of snapping off the head of the plant. This risk can be avoided by slipping the half-hitch knot on the wire while supporting the plant with the other hand. The string can then be spiralled round the stem beneath the leaves and re-secured in its former place. This progressive twisting of the plant should be carried out at roughly weekly intervals to prevent unruly growth.

It is a wise precaution, incidentally, to carry an extra string from around the middle of heavily laden plants to the wire to avoid loss due to failure of overtaxed strings.

Trimming is a more insistent job under glass than out of

Tomatoes in the Greenhouse

doors because growth is so much more rapid. Side shoots should be taken out just as soon as they can be handled and, where they do not snap away easily, a sharp knife should be used to make a clean cut.

The first few leaves near the pot will soon be overshadowed by those above, and they should be removed in easy stages by snapping them upwards while holding the main stem. In this way disease-susceptible tissue is removed and access to the pot for watering is facilitated.

Sometimes one finds that for no apparent reason a plant is growing away much more vigorously than the rest, and is, in fact, inclined to coarseness. Such a plant can best be steadied by allowing a second leader to develop and, with plants spaced at the desirable 18 inches apart, this extra shoot can be trained in without causing overcrowding. Once the growth has reached the wire the plants should be stopped by pinching out the growing point one leaf above the topmost truss. Under commercial conditions, with early planted crops, the growth is usually carried on and arched over the path, but in a small house this is seldom worth while and, in fact, it is of little use to allow further trusses to form after mid-August.

During the course of the season the foliage will tend to become heavily massed despite generous spacing of the plants. As free air circulation is all-important for maintaining strong trusses and reducing the incidence of disease, complete leaves should be removed here and there as required.

It is equally important, however, to retain as much as possible of the healthy foliage consistent with this free circulation of air. It is a common fallacy that the fruit will ripen more quickly if exposed to direct sunlight by removal of overshadowing leaves. (See also Chapter 2.)

There comes a time in most seasons—usually around mid-June—when every fallen bloom or dead piece of leaf develops a grey mass of Botrytis. This must be the sign to check the plants carefully, removing all tissue which is not fully active and healthy, and to give the plants a light dusting of sulphur, copper-lime dust or one of the newer proprietary fungicides, such as Folosan.

Copper preparations serve the additional purpose of checking leaf-mould, and if the dust is fogged into the space of the house very lightly once a week when the plants are damp in the early morning, little trouble with disease should be experienced.

General Notes

Throughout the growing season a constant watch should be kept for pests and diseases, since, under the protected conditions of greenhouse culture, infestation can be very rapid.

It is a recognized fact, however, and a fortunate one indeed, that pests and diseases which cause serious trouble to the commercial grower with his hundreds or thousands of plants are often unknown in the small amateur greenhouse. Thus, I have seldom needed to take positive measures against the most serious of commercial pests, red spider. Whitefly and greenfly turn up regularly and, with the minimum of heating, Botrytis disease is an ever-present menace.

On the other hand, I very rarely see leaf-mould disease, though on many a nursery it appears in June and seriously limits further cropping unless vigorous control measures are adopted.

It is as well, however, to bear in mind the troubles that can arise and, in this regard, reference should be made to the chapter on this subject.

Chapter 6

MODERN METHODS OF GROWING

While the soil is the natural rooting medium for the vast majority of plants, the artificial circumstance of greenhouse culture gives rise to soil fertility deterioration which is difficult if not impossible for the amateur to correct by the partial-sterilization techniques habitually adopted by the commercial grower.

It is well known that the growing of tomatoes or, indeed, of any other crop, year after year in the same greenhouse border soil leads to a progressive decline in yield despite generous manuring, fertilizing and adequate liming. This and other problems associated with soil growing have provided the incentive for devising methods of growing which can be relied upon to give consistently good results year after year.

The first advance in this direction, perfected from work carried out twenty years ago at a private research station in Sussex, is ring culture. The brief notes on this method which follow are intended to be an introduction to the detailed treatment provided in my book, *Ring Culture*, referred to in the Preface.

More recently has come straw-bale culture and the greater part of the present chapter is devoted to this novel, practical, and most effective means of overcoming the problems of soil deterioration under glass.

Modern Methods of Growing

RING CULTURE

This method of growing, particularly suited to tomatoes, involves planting in bottomless containers or 'rings' filled with J.I.P.3 or similar compost and standing on a bed of nutritionally-inert medium or 'aggregate' contained in a trough cut in the greenhouse border.

For the first few weeks the plants depend for both food and water upon the ring compost but thereafter rooting into the continually moist aggregate is encouraged. Feeding is limited entirely to the rings and the massive secondary root system developed in the aggregate becomes responsible for most of the water requirement of the plants.

This 'two-zone' root development with the ring roots taking up nutrient solution and the aggregate roots, unhampered by dissolved nutrients, absorbing water freely, enables maximum vigour to be maintained with a parallel strict control on fruit quality.

Ring culture has become the standard amateur method of growing tomatoes in the greenhouse and never fails to give first-rate results when correctly applied. Straw-bale culture may provide the first real challenge to this supremacy but has yet to become fully established.

STRAW-BALE CULTURE

A recent development in commercial tomato production, which has now been extended successfully to amateur growing, is straw-bale culture.

Basically, this involves causing the compressed straw composing the bale to ferment by saturation with water and the application of fertilizers, particularly of nitrogen, and setting the plants in a small bed or in mounds of soil compost applied to the surface. Heavy root development occurs in the rich,

72

moist organic matter of the decomposing straw, much as in the aggregate layer in ring culture, but as compared with the purely water-absorbing function of the aggregate roots, the bale roots are supplied with both water and nutrients as in normal soil growing.

As we know from our general gardening experience, straw is an excellent material for producing compost, as a big heap in thoroughly wet condition rapidly breaks down when a composting agent is incorporated. During this breaking down, especially over the first week or two, considerable heat is generated by the intense bacterial action and the high temperature is clearly apparent when a steaming forkful is dug out of the pile.

With loose straw such as this, the generation of heat is intense but short-lived, whereas in the compressed bale form slower decomposition can be contrived and heat is given off more gently over a longer period, though even here the peak temperature reached a few days after treatment often exceeds 120° F.

It will be seen, then, that a treated straw bale provides a source of gentle bottom heat as well as a highly fertile rooting medium, but this is not all. As raw organic matter, such as straw, breaks down, considerable quantities of carbon dioxide gas are given off. Research work of recent years has shown that the growth rate of many plants is increased considerably if the natural carbon dioxide level of the atmosphere is increased two- or threefold. In the instance of tomatoes, carbon dioxide enrichment of glasshouses is currently being practised on a considerable scale by using gas cylinders, solid carbon dioxide ('dry ice') or by burning propane gas. Crops are earlier to mature when other conditions of culture, such as temperature, are suitably adjusted and the increased returns much more than outweigh the cost of enrichment.

Although propane burners are now available for use in

Modern Methods of Growing

amateur greenhouses, carbon dioxide (CO_2) enrichment is not widely practised by gardeners as the technique of management of the greenhouse, particularly as regards ventilation, is too critical for worthwhile results to be obtained in most instances. When, however, the CO_2 is a by-product of the method of growing and costs nothing, the position is very different. The excellent results which commercial growers are achieving with straw-bale culture, and more recently amateur growers also 'are known to be due in part to this natural enrichment of the atmosphere of the growing quarters. There are obviously exciting possibilities in straw-bale growing in the amateur greenhouse and while the procedure is not yet fully cut and dried and ample room exists for personal experimentation, the general procedure has been well defined and adequately proved.

The details are as follows:

Bales of straw vary considerably in weight, according to method of production, and may scale as low as 40 lb. or as high as 80 lb. The fertilizer additions advised in commercial growing have been worked out per cwt. of substantially dry straw and a grower has no difficulty in working out the necessary application per bale according to the average weight of the bales which he buys in bulk. This is difficult for the gardener, however, and in my own trials of straw-bale culture, I have worked on the basis that a bale averages 56 lb. With a corresponding modification of the fertilizer quantities the results have been successful with a wide variety of bales and there is obviously sufficient latitude in the method to permit the quantities quoted below to be treated as standard.

In order to avoid possible contamination of the disease-free straw from the stale soil of the greenhouse, the bales should be stood on polythene sheeting—the ordinary 150 gauge used for greenhouse lining is suitable. It helps to retain moisture in the bales in the heat of summer if the polythene is used to line, and

74

Modern Methods of Growing

overlap by a few inches, a 2-inch deep trough cut in the green-house border to roughly the flat-side width of the bale.

The wire-tied bales (re-tie with strong wire if they are tied with string as bought, as string rots quickly) are laid closely end to end in the polythene-lined trough with the widest side horizontal and are then saturated with water. Straw, being tubular and shiny, tends to shed water, so saturation can be achieved only gradually. I find the best way is to apply 1 gallon of water per bale through a rosed can each day for 10–12 days.

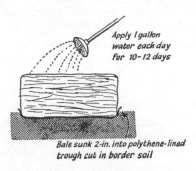

Apply 1 gallon water each day for 10–12 days

Bale sunk 2-in. into polythene-lined trough cut in border soil

Covering with polythene sheeting after each watering effectively prevents loss by evaporation in sunny weather. Some mould growth may appear on the straw under these conditions but this is not harmful.

At the end of the saturation period, ten days or so after taking the bales into the house, the compositing fertilizers are applied. The overall quantity of fertilizer to be applied to each bale depends upon the dry weight of the bale and the amounts of the individual fertilizers have been modified somewhat as the method has been perfected but, on the basis of a $\frac{1}{2}$ cwt. dry weight bale, I have found the following additions generally satisfactory:

75

1 lb. Nitrochalk

1 lb. superphosphate (I originally used twice this quantity but have since found it unnecessary)

1 lb. nitrate of potash (potassium nitrate)

4 oz. magnesium sulphate (Epsom salts)

3 oz. sulphate of iron.

These two latter additions are recent improvements which ensure that deficiencies of magnesium and iron will not normally develop. (See the note on this subject in Chapter 7.)

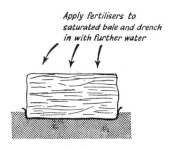

Apply fertilisers to saturated bale and drench in with further water

The fertilizers are each spread evenly over the surface of the bale and have then to be caused to penetrate into the straw as, left as a surface layer, their concentration would cause root damage. I find that the best way to achieve this penetration, without washing the more soluble materials right through, is to sprinkle over with about a gallon of water, allow half an hour for the Nitrochalk to soften, rub over the treated surface with the flat of a spade, and then to apply a further gallon of water.

Intense bacterial activity will now commence and in a heated greenhouse the internal temperature of the bale rises rapidly. In an unheated house early in the year heating up may be slow and it is best to re-cover the bale loosely with the polythene

Modern Methods of Growing

sheeting for a few days. Make sure that the bale remains thoroughly moist by sprinkling as necessary.

After a few days, the planting bed or individual mounds can be placed on the bale surface to warm up. This is the usual procedure but, to make watering easier as the season advances, I prefer to contain the planting compost in bottomless composition pots, or rings, as in ring culture. J.I.P.3 is a suitable compost, whether applied direct to the bale or in rings, but I also have good reports of various soilless composts, including Levington compost, and I suggest that a comparative trial be made.

Roughly 1 gallon of compost is required for each plant and an individual bale will accommodate two tomato plants though, if two bales are placed end to end, five plants can be set out without overcrowding.

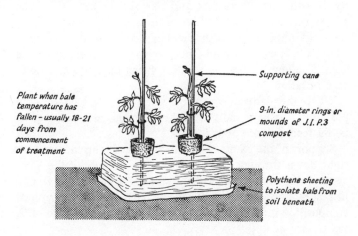

Plant when bale temperature has fallen – usually 18-21 days from commencement of treatment

Supporting cane

9-in. diameter rings or mounds of J.I. P.3 compost

Polythene sheeting to isolate bale from soil beneath

Planting can be safely undertaken when the internal temperature of the bale has fallen to 100 degrees but as most gardeners do not have a suitable thermometer for pushing into the straw, I suggest using a cane or stick pushed in deeply as a temperature indicator. When, after being left in for at least an hour, the buried portion of the stick on being withdrawn feels only slightly warm to the hand, the temperature is safe.

The general cultural requirements of the crop are little different from those described for border or ring culture. It is, however, essential to keep the straw thoroughly moist by frequent sprinkling or, as the season progresses, heavy watering.

Feeding should commence a fortnight after planting and this primarily involves applying ¼ lb. Nitrochalk per bale evenly spread and watered, on three or four occasions at fortnightly intervals. By this means nitrogen deficiency in the straw is avoided and the bale continues to give off gentle heat over a prolonged period. Normal liquid feeding will be required alternately with the Nitrochalk and this should be with a high potash tomato liquid fertilizer such as Boots Compure K at standard dilution or with the home-made feed detailed in Chapter 7. It will be found that the vigour of growth justifies at least 2 gallons of feeding solution being applied per bale on each occasion.

Where the plants are set in rings stood on the bale, the compost must be kept moist and should be given a share of the liquid feed on each occasion.

Support of the plants can be by means of long canes pushed right down through the compost and bale or by the string system with an open tie to the lower stem of each plant. In both instances, however, the natural sinkage of the bale during decomposition must be allowed for by occasional slacking of the ties or strings.

The only other cultural variation in straw-bale growing concerns ventilation. Since the uptake by the plants of the extra CO_2 given off by the decomposing straw is really active only when the temperature is above 60 degrees, it is desirable not to open the house ventilators until around 75 degrees is reached. Once the ventilators are opened, of course, the evolved CO_2 is rapidly lost. This applies up to around mid-June. Thereafter full ventilation both night and day is more beneficial in the direction of disease-avoidance than anything which might be gained by the waning evolution of CO_2.

Finally, it should be noted that results scarcely less spectacular than with straw-bale culture as such are being achieved commercially where, instead of using entire bales, 'straw wads' beds are made up to 6 to 8 inches deep by cutting the ties and separating the wads of which the bale is composed.

In this case the pre-wetting and fertilizing procedure is all proportionate per unit area; in other words, if the wad bed is the same width and half as deep as a bale, the length will be twice as great and the whole length should receive the quantities indicated for a bale. Feeding, however, should be on the same scale since as many plants will be accommodated but on a more shallow depth of straw.

Straw-bale or, indeed, straw-wad, culture can also be employed for outdoor tomato production.

The general procedure is identical with that described for the greenhouse but, even with polythene sheet draping during the soaking period, the temperature rise in the straw will be less marked than under the protection of glass. The best results will be obtained where a warm corner is chosen for siting the bales or wads and, with bales, rapid drying of the straw should be minimized by encircling with polythene firmly tied lengthwise into position. Mound beds will also be found less subject to drying out than rings stood on the straw surface.

The only hazard with straw-bale or wad culture is the possible contamination of the straw with one or other of the highly persistent selective weedkillers which are being used to an increasing extent by farmers of corn crops. Residues of these weedkillers in the straw can cause severe distortion and virtual failure of the plants, but short of seeking out a farmer who does not use these weedkillers and who is prepared to supply a bale or two of his 'clean' straw, there is nothing for it but to buy from the local corn merchant and take a chance with his frequently mixed and unidentifiable supply.

Compared with ring culture, straw-bale growing is still in the advanced developmental stage but it is an extremely promising way of growing heavy crops of high quality fruit and I suggest that it be tried on one side of the greenhouse in comparison with border growing or ring culture on the other.

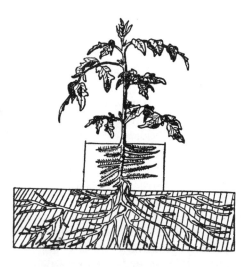

Diagrammatic representation of ring culture

Chapter 7

FEEDING

B roadly speaking, feeding constitutes supplying a plant's
nutrient requirements right from the time that the seed
germinates and a root is produced until growth is com.
pleted at the end of the season. By common usage, however,
this term has come to mean the application of fertilizers during
the main cropping period of the plant to supplement the food
reserve present in the soil or compost at planting time.

The details of feeding depend to some extent upon the system
adopted. Thus, plants set out in deep, rich border soil in the
greenhouse will need less feeding for an equivalent crop than
those grown by ring culture where the only reserve of food is
supplied by the relatively small amount of compost in the ring.
Whatever the system, however, the principle is the same inas-
much as the tomato is a heavy feeder and needs generous
treatment to develop a full crop.

The balance of the feed, i.e. the relative content of nitrogen,
phosphoric acid and potash, has a considerable influence upon
the quality of growth. The phosphoric acid appears to have the
least influence since, although adequate supplies of phosphates
are required for promoting strong root action, good truss
development and even-setting of the blooms, the amount
present in the fertilizers added to the border soil, container,
compost or straw substrate is practically sufficient for the requirements throughout the cropping period. On the other hand,

Feeding

the balance between nitrogen and potash is the deciding factor in determining the quality of growth.

A plant amply supplied with potash and only just enough nitrogen to allow the fruit to develop normally and extension growth to continue steadily, produces a heavy crop of well-coloured, firm and generally high quality fruit. For that reason we feed with an emphasis on potash, at least until the growth has been thoroughly steadied by the weight of fruit, and only later is the balance changed in favour of nitrogen to maintain extension growth and to enable the higher trusses to continue normal development despite the demands of the crop on the lower trusses.

This, broadly, is the basic principle of tomato feeding and we have now to consider the practical details.

The first point to bear in mind is that overfeeding is a much commoner fault than underfeeding. A partly starved plant merely fails to give a full crop, but one which is given too much feed usually dies outright because the root system is so burnt up that neither food nor water can be absorbed.

So much is established fact which any gardener can prove to his own satisfaction or regret if he wishes. There is nothing so clear cut, however, about the best way of feeding from the point of view of type of feed, quantity to apply and frequency of application.

Every experienced gardener has his own ideas on the 'right' way of feeding any particular crop, but these ways are so diverse that the newcomer to gardening can be excused for wondering whether there is such a thing as a right way of feeding.

The answer is that circumstances of soil, cultivation and climate are so variable that discretion and experience are factors inseparable from the successful application of any feed or method of feeding.

However, in container culture, we have adopted positive

measures to standardize the factors of soil and cultivation and have ruled out to some extent the disturbing factors of climate. Consequently, fairly definite advice can be given on feeding in the knowledge that the results will be satisfactory.

I have studied this important matter in considerable detail over the years, and have come to the definite conclusion that feeding in liquid form has considerable advantages over application of solid fertilizers. By this I do not mean the use of the odorous proceeds of the old-fashioned manure/soot tub, but rather the carefully balanced, quickly available liquid fertilizers or soluble-solid mixtures of comparable type which are so rapidly gaining popularity with the gardener as well as with the commercial grower.

Liquid fertilizers bought as concentrated solutions in tins or bottles are merely diluted with water as required. The solids have to be dissolved in water to produce the fertilizer solution. In either case, some simple form of measure is indicated or provided, and the instructions for use include advice on how much to use for any given quantity of water.

Whereas the ordinary run of tomato fertilizers bought in packets for application in solid form are composed largely of ingredients which do not dissolve in water, those applied as liquids are carried wherever the water penetrates and so feed all the roots effectively and rapidly. Much of the insoluble part of solid fertilizers is organic in nature and this tends to accumulate on the surface of the soil with the formation of an air-excluding scum.

Fertilizers in solution, on the other hand, have no such effect and, as all the ingredients are available to the roots, they are much more economical to use than solids. Their cost per unit is higher than solids, however, and consequently the outlay per plant is much the same in either case, but the results in terms of balanced, fruitful growth are greatly in favour of liquid fertilizers.

Feeding

My original work on liquid feeding tomatoes and other crops was based on a range of liquid fertilizers identified as '667', '665' and '853', the numbers referring to the percentage contents of nitrogen, phosphoric acid and potash respectively. At one time available to gardeners through retailers, I understand that these are now supplied only by Monro Horticultural Sundries Ltd., Waltham Cross, Herts.

In this revision of the text, these fertilizers are still featured since they are indicative of the balance of feeding which experience has shown to be particularly suitable for tomatoes at various stages of growth. Widely available alternatives which I can thoroughly recommend are PBI 'Topglass' with an analysis of 5 per cent nitrogen, 5 per cent phosphoric acid, 8 per cent potash (5, 5, 8), and Maxicrop Tomato Special with an analysis of 5·1, 5·1, 6·7.

As with 667, Topglass has a content of magnesium while Maxicrop, based on an extract of seaweed, is claimed to have a natural content of all trace elements as well as of the main nutrients, nitrogen, phosphoric acid and potash. Under certain circumstances, otherwise fertile soils may be unable fully to satisfy the trace element requirements of strong growing, heavy fruiting plants, such as the tomato, and Maxicrop is likely in these cases to give superior results, particularly in regard to fruit flavour and general quality.

Topglass and Maxicrop are supplied with specific advice on rate of dilution and application under various circumstances, including ring culture. I have, however, used both at the higher strengths indicated for 667 in the following pages with excellent results, so it is, perhaps, a question of trying out various strengths for oneself and deciding which routine of feeding best suits one's own way of growing.

At the end of this chapter will be found details for making up feeds along 'do-it-yourself' lines. Since I first worked these out and applied them some ten years ago, with publication a year or

Feeding

two later, they have been widely used with unqualified success.

The amount of feed and frequency of application are factors dependent upon the system of culture, and it will make for easy reference if these various aspects are considered according to the main cultural systems.

In the Greenhouse Border Soil

In this instance the customary generous preparation of the soil prior to planting will have ensured considerable reserves of food and neither frequent nor heavy feeding is usually required to produce a good crop, especially where the plants are not set out until April.

I find it satisfactory to apply half a fluid ounce (1 medicinal tablespoonful) of 667 per plant mixed into a gallon of water and applied at ten-day intervals.

The first feed should be given when the first fruits on the bottom truss are the size of a walnut. In order to avoid any danger of root scorch, the soil should be in a moist condition and I find it best to water normally the day before feeding. This routine gives excellent results with most varieties during the greater part of the growing season.

Sometimes, however, although this feed has fair emphasis on potash, the growth shows signs of becoming too vigorous; the trusses are inclined to be widely separated and instead of standing out strongly from the stem, tend to be erect and much branched. This can come about as a result of prolonged dull weather, over-watering, or the use of too much nitrogen as manure or in the base fertilizer prior to planting.

Should there be signs of this type of growth the plants must be steadied with a purely potash feed. For this purpose I make up a potash liquid feed by adding 2 lb. sulphate of potash to a gallon of water in a pail and stirring occasionally over a period of a couple of days or so. Only part dissolves, but the solution becomes saturated. This solution is now used instead of a feed of 667 and at the same ½ fl. oz. rate.

It may be necessary to give more than one purely potash feed in this manner to produce the desirable blue-green colour of foliage and perfect ripening of the fruit. There is, however, a danger with continued potash feeding that magnesium deficiency will develop, with the typical yellow blotching of the leaves around the third and fourth truss. To prevent this, each plant should be given a level tablespoonful of magnesium sulphate (Epsom salts) once a month in between the other feeds.

By the time the plant is carrying five or six well-formed trusses of fruit, the vigour of growth will be much less and a change from 667 to a higher nitrogen and lower potash feed is desirable to swell the upper fruit and to keep the plant growing. For this purpose I use a liquid fertilizer in the same range, known as '853'; the same amount and rate of dilution applies, and the effect on a somewhat weary plant is very marked.

By mid-August, feeding can cease since from then on the remaining fruit can develop with the reserves already supplied.

In the Garden or Allotment

Where the plants are being grown by the time-honoured method in the open soil, feeding can follow exactly the same lines as detailed above for greenhouse border culture.

Since one is growing under natural conditions and in the normal season, however, additional potash feeds are needed only in periods of soft, dull weather.

The 667 feed every ten days gives excellent results, but it is worth while to use the extra magnesium advised above.

Ring Culture in the Greenhouse or Out of Doors

This system was developed with the use of 667 liquid fertilizer and apart from the occasional need for extra potash feeding if the plants tend to be too vigorous, and a regular addition of extra magnesium, this fertilizer has proved to be entirely adequate.

It will have been noted in Chapter 6 that a fundamental part of the system is the restriction of all feeding to the ring compost. For best effects, we try to avoid the feeds draining down into the aggregate and, to this end, the ½ fl. oz. feeds are mixed with less water. It has been shown that the 14 lb. or so of J.I.P. compost in a 9-inch container will retain almost exactly 3 pints of liquid if application is made when the compost is still just nicely moist.

The routine, then, is to dilute the 667 at the rate of 1½ fl. oz. to just over a gallon of water and to divide this amount among three plants. Since, however, the whole food supply of the plant depends upon the nutrients in this quite small amount of compost, it is necessary to feed every six to seven days.

The same details apply where it is necessary to give a purely potash feed, while for additional magnesium I find it best to give a teaspoonful per plant once a fortnight with a light watering.

A changeover to 853 when the plants are heavy with fruit may prove desirable, but all the while growth is steady and the higher trusses are setting freely the use of 667 can continue.

Incidentally, it should be noted that since under correct ring culture conditions the compost remains moist between feeds due to suction from the aggregate, there is no need to water prior to feeding. If in doubt, however, a pint or so of water a few hours before feeding will do no harm.

Straw-Bale Culture

Details of the feeding procedure found to be suitable with this latest method of growing are included in Chapter 6. It should be noted particularly that, by reason of the large bulk of straw involved, feeding requirements are higher than by other methods of growing and under-feeding is a more likely fault than undue generosity.

In Containers standing on a Hard Surface

In this instance, the plant depends entirely on the compost not only for nutrient supplies, but also for water. Feeding with 667 at ring culture strength is likely to check the uptake of water unduly with consequent restriction of growth, and I have found it better to use half the strength of feed twice a week. This means 1½ fl. oz. of 667 in just over 2 gallons of water, 3 pints of solution being given to each plant every third or fourth day.

With the compost drying out rapidly and needing watering practically every day in hot weather, I find this feeding routine most satisfactory and an almost incredible crop can be grown in relation to the restricted root-run.

In Containers standing upon the Border Soil

Here we have the feeding roots divided between the compost in the container and the border. I find that a satisfactory way of feeding is to use ½ fl. oz. of 667 diluted with a gallon of water for each plant divided between the compost in the container and the surrounding border soil. The compost should be in moist condition prior to feeding. The details of extra potash and magnesium feeds apply as for plants grown entirely in the border.

For those who like to make up their ring culture feed at home from easily-obtained ingredients, the following has proved a good and relatively inexpensive substitute for 667.

Feeding

In parts by weight (ounces or pounds)—

> 4 parts nitrate of potash
> 10 parts superphosphate
> 5 parts sulphate of ammonia
> 7 parts magnesium sulphate (Epsom salts).

Keep the mixture completely dry by excluding air and use 1½ oz. per gallon of water to make up the ring feed. Thorough stirring is necessary to effect solution and even then there is a portion, derived from the superphosphate, which will not dissolve but this need cause no concern as it does not affect the strength of the feed. Don't worry if the solution is cloudy; this is quite in order. Use at the rate of 2½ pints to each ring every 7 days or, even better, at 1 pint to each ring every third day.

A softer end-of-season feed, equivalent to 853, also used at the rate of 1½ oz. per gallon, is made up of:

> 1 part nitrate of potash
> 4 parts superphosphate
> 5 parts sulphate of ammonia
> 4 parts magnesium sulphate.

Occasionally the young top growth of the plants takes on a sickly, yellow mottled or almost bleached appearance. This is usually due to a deficiency of iron and is most likely to occur with heavily-laden ring culture plants on an aggregate other than cinder ash and with plants restricted entirely to containers.

Correction of these symptoms can often be achieved by applying Murphy Sequestrene according to the label directions. If, however, no improvement occurs after a week or so, the trouble is probably of virus rather than trace element origin and is incapable of being corrected.

Chapter 8

PESTS AND DISEASES

Gardening books as a whole seem to deal with the subject of plant parasites in one of two ways. Either pests
and diseases are presented as waging a relentless war
which the gardener can combat only by spending a great deal
more money on sprays and dusts, and time in applying them,
than the plants are worth from any point of view or, as by the
'organic' extremists, as something to be ignored into non-
existence. Both, to my mind, are wrong.

Thus, it is no less foolish to ignore the enemy than to reckon
his defeat an end in itself.

After quite a number of years of experience of this subject, I
have verified to my own satisfaction only one general fact: that
a healthy, well-grown plant, be it a tomato or a rose, is less
likely to be adversely affected by insect pest or fungus disease
attack than one which is battling against poor culture. No more
and no less.

What does this mean as far as our culture of the tomato is
concerned? It means that the more trouble we take in *growing*
the plants, the less time we shall need to spend in *protecting or
curing* them.

On the other hand, we must recognize that weather conditions are beyond our control and that conditions which check
the normal flow of growth are the ally of the parasite.

So, however well we are growing the crop, it pays to know

Pests and Diseases

the enemy and to have the knowledge for defence or attack as the case may be.

Outdoor plants are subject to attack by a shorter list of pests than those grown under the more artificial conditions of the greenhouse, but when it comes to fungus diseases there is, curiously enough, little to choose.

Pests can be dealt with once they are first noticed, whereas diseases are far more easily prevented than controlled so we will deal with the easiest problem first.

PESTS

Aphides or Greenfly

Few plants escape the attentions of one or more types of this large and various-coloured family of plant lice, and tomatoes, both outdoors and under glass, are often attacked at the young stages. Strongly growing plants are seldom troubled, but those which are checked by bad culture or unfavourable weather conditions are further weakened and prompt control measures are necessary. The young leaves are covered by the sticky excrement of the insects, the puncturing during feeding causes distortion of growth and misshapen fruits are often the result of greenfly punctures at the setting or early development stages.

Fortunately, aphides are easily controlled by any one of a number of old and new specifics. Derris, in either dust or liquid form, is an old remedy but still one of the best since it is non-poisonous to the user and works effectively at temperatures too low for that other garden standby, nicotine.

The modern insecticide BHC, preferably in its pure non-tainting lindane form, is also most effective under the relatively low spring temperatures, but it is inclined to harden somewhat and so is not advisable at the propagating stages. The well-known insecticide, DDT, though very useful for controlling other pests is, contrary to commonly given advice, almost useless against aphides.

In the greenhouse, with the higher temperatures which prevail even in the early season, nicotine fumigating shreds are commonly used against greenfly in its various forms. These shreds are convenient because the amount employed on each occasion can be regulated to suit the volume of the house to a fairly exact degree, so that poor effects from underdosing or damage due to overdosing can be avoided.

Once the plants are past the seedling and young stages, lindane smokes are generally preferred due to the greater persistency of this insecticide. Repeat fumigations should be made whenever the pest is again observed but, providing the first attack is dealt with promptly, one fumigation is often sufficient to keep the plants clean.

Leaf Miner

The maggots of the leaf miner fly tunnel between the upper and lower leaf surfaces and give rise to the unmistakable twisting white lines which are clearly visible against the surrounding green of the leaf.

Where this pest has been present on greenhouse-grown plants, it is not unusual to find the next year's seedlings or young plants heavily attacked. Under normal conditions, the soil of the house in which tomatoes are to be propagated is always sterilized by steaming to kill the overwintering stage of the pest. We cannot do this in the small greenhouse and the best procedure in preparation for propagation is to wash down the house thoroughly with disinfectant and to replace with fertile garden soil the top 3 or 4 inches of the greenhouse border which is harbouring the overwintering cocoons.

If tiny white spots followed by white tunnels appear on the seed leaves or first rough leaves, 3 per cent nicotine dust should be applied lightly when the temperature is 60° F. or above. This usually checks the attack and may eradicate the pest completely.

If the damage persists, however, as the plants are growing away in the 3-inch pots or soil blocks, a lindane spray application will be required, and this kills the maggots in the mines as well as preventing further egg-laying by the flies. As previously stated, this insecticide tends to harden the growth of seedlings or very young plants, hence the early use of nicotine, but I have used lindane smokes as early as the pricking-out stage without apparent damage and with complete eradication of the pest.

Attacks which develop during the growing season should be dealt with on outdoor plants by lindane spraying and in the greenhouse by lindane smoke fumigation. Safe and effective forms of both are readily available at garden shops.

TOMATO MOTH

The caterpillars of this pest, which are usually green when young and brown when mature, attack the leaves, stem and fruit, and can cause a serious loss of crop. The eggs are laid in clusters on the underneath side of the leaves and, unless one happens to be on the look-out for these egg masses, the first sign of the pest is a leaf eaten away to a skeleton almost overnight by dozens of tiny caterpillars. They grow rapidly, crawl to further leaves and can cause havoc if not controlled.

The old-established, but objectionable, spraying with the poisonous lead arsenate has now been entirely superseded by DDT in some form. Out of doors, light dusting of the plants with 5 per cent DDT, preferably when the foliage is moist with dew, is quickly and completely effective.

The same measure can be employed in the greenhouse where, incidentally, the pest is much more likely to be troublesome than out of doors, or DDT smoke fumigation can be employed.

Pests and Diseases

WHITEFLY

Another essentially greenhouse pest, though in some south-western areas it is occasionally found on outdoor plants. These tiny moth-like insects exude a honey dew upon which grows a black mould. The growth of the plant is checked, due to blocking of the breathing pores, and the fruit requires to be washed and wiped. This again is an uncommon pest in these days, as DDT in any convenient form has proved such an effective control.

In the greenhouse DDT smoke fumigation provides the most convenient control, but, with established attacks, application should be repeated three times at four- or five-day intervals, as the eggs are not killed by the insecticide.

RED SPIDER MITE

Another pest limited almost entirely to the greenhouse crop, though in hot, dry weather it sometimes appears on outdoor plants, particularly if growth is stunted and unhealthy. The tiny spider-like creatures which, incidentally, are brownish in colour and only red at the hibernating stage in autumn, are concentrated on the under-surface of the leaves and cause a white speckling of the foliage.

If an attack is allowed to develop, webs are spun beneath the leaves and from leaf to leaf until the whole of the young growth of the plant is enveloped and cropping is severely checked.

The old-established method of control, involving spraying with a petroleum oil emulsion, such as Volck, is still unequalled providing the spray is thoroughly and forcefully applied.

The pest can, however, be kept in check by routine fumigation with the non-poisonous azobenzene smoke. To be effective, however, this material requires a temperature of around 70° F.

during the period of an overnight fumigation. Consequently it is only really useful to the amateur during the summer months, and Volck is to be preferred earlier in the season.

SLUGS AND SNAILS

Every garden seems to have its quota of these 'natives' and, though they prefer sweeter foliage than the pungent tomato, young plants may be seriously damaged. Mainly outdoor pests, although a watch must be kept for them in the greenhouse, especially at the propagating stage.

Fortunately the solid fuel, metaldehyde, is both attractive and fatal to slugs and snails. Small heaps of the familiar metaldehyde/bran bait should be placed near the plants as soon as they are set out and, at the first sign of the typical slimy trails in the greenhouse, the young plants should be similarly protected. It is as well to keep the bait off the actual boxes or pots as, though the metaldehyde is not a plant poison, the decay of the bran encourages damping-off diseases. Liquid slug baits are now available and these metaldehyde suspensions merely require to be diluted according to instructions and sprinkled lightly over the plants. Since these notes were first written, pellets composed of metaldehyde dispersed in an attractant base have largely superseded the loose bait. Such pellets can be scattered indiscriminately without risk of plant damage.

WOODLICE

Mainly a pest of the young plants in the greenhouse and during the hardening-off period in the cold frame. Seedlings are eaten off at ground level while older ones may be weakened or killed by damage to the lower stem.

Woodlice are susceptible to DDT, and dusting around the boxes, pots or set-out plants with a 5 per cent dust gives effective protection. The dust should, however, be kept off the actual plants as considerable hardening may occur at the young stages.

Leaf Hoppers

These pale green, active insects frequently attack the seedling plants and cause a speckled white or bleached appearance of the seed leaves. The pest itself is often difficult to find during the daytime, but the type of damage and the presence of white, cast skins of the immature stages on the under-surfaces of the leaves serve as identification. Nicotine dusting or fumigation with nicotine shreds, under warm conditions, deals with hoppers safely and effectively.

With older plants lindane smoke fumigation is satisfactory.

Soil Pests

By baking the loam fraction of the compost we avoid trouble from soil pests at the propagating stages, but plants in the greenhouse border or out of doors may be attacked by several types.

On land recently broken up from grass, WIREWORM may do serious damage by eating the roots and tunnelling up into the stem.

Under weed-infested, neglected conditions, CUTWORMS and LEATHERJACKETS often abound and these pests eat away the stem tissues at ground level and cause collapse of the plants.

The familiar MILLIPEDE which curls up when touched and its tiny relative, the SYMPHILID or WHITE INSECT, are occasional pests of plants grown in the greenhouse soil. Roots are eaten away and the plants may become blue and stunted.

All of these lurking enemies can be killed or deterred from attacking the plants either by working lindane wireworm dust

Young plants in a home-made propagator

The same plants a month later

Soil sterilization by baking

Moneymaker in the Benington ring culture trial. Gravel/cinder aggregate

Ring culture at Benington shortly after planting

into the soil before planting or by watering individual plants with a lindane spray concentrate diluted according to instructions. It is important, however, not to exceed the recommended rate with either the dust or liquid as, even in its pure, lindane form, BHC can check the growth of young plants.

DISEASES

Compared with the modern range of insecticides there are still comparatively few materials which can be used safely to combat fungus diseases and none to effect a cure of a plant affected by a virus disorder. This is perhaps understandable when it is appreciated that a fungus growth is a primitive plant and, as such, is much closer in nature to the plant it attacks than an insect pest. Thus, the margin between killing the disease and sparing the plant and killing both is usually very narrow.

When it comes to a virus disease the infection is so much a part of the actual plant that the problem is even more difficult. At present, all we can do is to check the spread of viruses by controlling insects, such as aphides, which carry the infection from one plant to another. In view of these facts, much of what follows will be seen to concern prevention of attack rather than cure.

Damping-off

This is a condition of the seedling and the young plant in which the stem tissue shrivels at or near ground level and the growth collapses. It is caused by one or other of a group of several fungi which can live in the soil and whose spores or 'seeds' can be airborne from external sources of infection.

Prevention of this common trouble involves using a clean compost, i.e. one in which the soil portion has been sterilized, by cleaning down the greenhouse and sterilizing the soil of the

97

house before propagating starts, by sowing thinly to prevent drawn, weak seedlings and by using the well-known Cheshunt Compound before and after sowing.

This material is a copper preparation which is used by dissolving 1 oz. in 2 gallons of water in an enamelled—not a metal —pail and applying the solution to the seed-boxes to the extent of a thorough sprinkling by means of a rosed can made of copper or an ordinary can where the metal has become covered over the years with a limey deposit. These precautions are necessary, since the strength of the solution is rapidly lost when in contact with metals other than copper itself.

Application before sowing usually prevents the trouble, but further freshly-made solution can be applied at the first signs of any seedlings falling over. At this stage it is wise to follow the application with a light sprinkling of plain water to prevent the delicate foliage being scorched when the solution dries.

The same method can be used to protect young plants at the early potting stages, and then a light surface watering on moist soil is a suitable method.

I have given a fair amount of detail on this subject, as damping-off is undoubtedly the most serious trouble encountered by any gardener who sets out to raise his own plants.

'Blight' Disease

Generally limited to the outdoor crop, but one occasionally troublesome in the greenhouse late in the year.

Most gardeners associate blight with potatoes and, indeed, it is the same disease which attacks these two closely allied crops. In warm, wet spells of weather in the late summer, black areas may develop on the leaves while the fruit is also attacked and rots completely. To reduce the likelihood of attack, tomatoes should not be grown near a potato crop, and close planting with the consequent heavily massed foliage, should be avoided.

Pests and Diseases

I have never experienced this disease with plants grown in containers against a wall or other protecting structure. This is probably due to the free circulation of air and the better balance of growth which results from this method.

At the first signs of the disease the plants should be sprayed from top to bottom with a copper compound, such as Bordeaux mixture or colloidal copper. I prefer the latter, as it causes less marking of the fruit and less hardening of growth. The addition of a horticultural wetting agent or oil spray, such as Volck, is desirable to ensure thorough wetting of all surfaces and further applications should be given at 7–10 day intervals.

Definitely a disease to be taken at the early stages, as it can be a killer.

Phytophthora and Didymella Stem Rots

These diseases may cause death of the plant at all stages from planting to maturity, but the former is a damping-off type of disease causing shrivelling of the stem tissue near ground level and is usually associated with the early season.

Didymella causes sunken areas on the stem, usually near ground level, and the plant is rapidly killed. The disease is distinguished by the presence of tiny black spore-cases or pycnidia which appear on the dead tissue. It may also attack higher up the plant, and out of doors it causes a rot of the fruit. Under glass the fruit is seldom attacked.

There is no cure for either of these troubles, but, with sterilized soil or clean compost and good air circulation, they are seldom troublesome to the gardener. Affected plants should be removed completely and burnt at once.

Botrytis

A disease which causes a rotting of the stem, of the fruit at the calyx end and of damaged leaves. Affected parts develop a heavy ash-grey mould which readily distinguishes this disease. Mainly troublesome in the greenhouse and only of significance out of doors under crowded conditions.

The disease enters the stem through stumps of leaves and shoots left by careless trimming, and consequently all cuts should be made flush to the stem.

Diseased fruits should be removed and burnt before they cause rotting of surrounding fruits; diseased leaves should be cut out hard to the stem and attacked areas on the stem should be cut out with a sharp knife back to clean tissue and the wound protected with a paste made up of the proprietary product Folosan and water. This dust fungicide is also most useful under glass for fogging into the air of the greenhouse to in-activate the spores which arise in clouds from the diseased areas, and so prevent the trouble spreading. The harder and better the balance of growth the less trouble will there be from Botrytis.

Leaf Mould

This disease, caused by the fungus *Cladosporium fulvum*, is of serious concern to commercial growers in many areas, but, curiously enough, very seldom appears in the amateur green-house—neither is it a disease of the outdoor crop. It need not, therefore, concern us greatly, but it is as well to be able to recognize it.

Late in the season, usually under damp, stagnant conditions, a furry mould, at first light in colour but turning to olive brown, appears on the under-surface of the leaves. As the mould develops, yellow patches appear on the upper surface and, if the attack is not checked, the leaf curls up and shrivels.

If the crop is well developed the leaves can be removed completely as they show signs of attack, but earlier on the plants should be thoroughly sprayed at 10-day intervals with normally diluted Volck to which colloidal copper has been added at the rate indicated on the label of the type purchased.

It is, of course, of prime importance to wet the under-surface of the leaves, whether infected or healthy, when spraying against leaf mould, and a syringe provided with an up-turned nozzle is necessary.

Verticillium Wilt

A common disease of both greenhouse and outdoor plants and one frequently contracted from the propagating soil and 'bought in' with the plants. The growth of the fungus in the lower stem tissues impedes the flow of sap and the foliage wilts heavily in hot weather. The disease may not be apparent until the plant is heavily laden with fruit, but the sharply down-turned lower foliage with a consequent 'bunchy' effect is an easily recognized early symptom. Another diagnostic feature of this disease is the brown appearance of the 'wood' tissue when the bark of the lower stem is sliced with a knife.

If a plant wilts heavily in the daytime but recovers in the cool of the evening, *Verticillium* should be suspected and, if the 'wood' is brown, the whole plant including the root should be burned—not thrown on the compost heap to introduce infection the following season.

VIRUS DISEASES

These have been described as disorders of the plant and they can be recognized only by the symptoms they cause. The commonest tomato virus, Mosaic, gives rise to a yellow mottling and slight crinkling of the leaves, while yellowish streaks may appear on the young extension growth. The plants are more or less stunted, and failure of the trusses to develop normally, or loss of the blooms before setting, cause a reduction in the crop.

Nothing can be done to cure such plants and they should be pulled out and burned as soon as any worth-while fruit has ripened. In the meantime, infected plants should always be handled last during any operation of trimming and twisting, as the virus can be transferred on the fingers or knife. Further reference to this large and complex subject will be found in *Tomato Growing*.

From the practical point of view, the best insurance against trouble with virus infections is to purchase plants from a local nurseryman who takes pains to avoid introducing infection or, when raising one's own plants, to observe a strict routine of hygiene and pest control and to avoid touching the plants at any time after handling tobacco. The point here is that several virus disorders are common to both tobacco and tomato plants, and there is often active virus in pipe and cigarette tobacco.

Chapter 9

VARIETIES

S eed catalogues present a bewildering choice of tomato varieties, each with a glowing description which is hard to resist. Many are undoubtedly very good and some are particularly suitable for certain types of soil, climate and cultivation.

From my experience, however, the gardener is most likely to be satisfied with the results of his efforts if the choice is one of the prominent market varieties which have stood the test of time. The mere fact that a variety has become established in the face of the critical requirements of commercial culture stamps it with the qualities of reliability and freedom of cropping under conditions far removed from individual attention.

Such a variety, treated with the extra care which our small number of plants allows, seldom fails to respond effectively despite widely varying conditions of culture.

This versatility of standard varieties is well demonstrated by the fact that many a market grower successfully employs the same variety both in his heated glasshouses and in the field. Admittedly few varieties respond satisfactorily to the forcing conditions required for the production of really early fruit and *Potentate*, for all its faults of poor quality, has for long been the early growers' choice, and even to-day has not been completely superseded. From our point of view, however, the suitability of a variety for forcing is of no consequence since the high fuel expenditure required with early work is quite uneconomic under amateur conditions.

After working with a wide range of varieties over the years I have yet to find one more generally acceptable than *Stonor's Moneymaker*.

Planted in the greenhouse in March/April with a modest amount of artificial heat it provides a heavy crop of excellent quality fruit from mid-June onwards. It is, by general consent, the ideal variety for the controlled conditions of ring culture and, providing there is emphasis on potash until growth is controlled by the fruit, the tendency for excess vigour and consequent small, hollow or poorly coloured fruit can be avoided.

Out of doors it sets fruit as well as any variety, while the typically pale green fruit ripens with a thinner skin than one normally associates with garden culture. A strong, searching root system allows it to flourish when weaker rooters, such as *Potentate*, fail miserably. I have found it no more susceptible to leaf mould under glass than *Potentate* or *Ailsa Craig*, or to blight diseases out of doors than the specially raised open-air varieties such as *Carter's Sunrise*, *Harbinger*, *Hundredfold* and *Early Market*.

Strain is certainly an important consideration with *Moneymaker* as with any other variety, however. I have encountered crops of this variety where the fruit was by no means as uniform and smooth as it should be and where a wild, poor-setting habit had crept in. There is no excuse for this as it is the easiest of varieties to select for trueness to type, but it is wise to buy the seed from the raisers, Messrs. F. Stonor Ltd., St. Margaret's Nurseries, Brook Lane, Sarisbury Green, Hants, or at least from a seed firm of the highest reputation.

Moneymaker has been criticized on the score that it ripens more slowly than others such as *Potentate* and the John Innes hybrid *Ware Cross*. Certainly the bottom truss is inclined to be slow in colouring but, so far as we are concerned, this is

Varieties

offset by the steady flow of fruit coming, as often as not, from three trusses at the same time.

Great claims have been made for the rapid maturing habit and outstanding cropping capacity of this and that fancy variety, but I have yet to encounter one which seriously challenges the established favourites. It should, however, be recorded that bush varieties such as *Puck*, *The Amateur* and the very dwarf, *Atom*, resulting largely from earlier breeding work at the John Innes Horticultural Institution, have a precocity and abundance of fruiting which does much to compensate for the rather small size and mediocre quality of the fruit.

These varieties are worth growing in the generously prepared soil of a warm border and with the early protection of barn-type cloches, for the sake of some early fruit. The more or less prostrate habit requires that the fruit be lifted clear of the soil by means of side strings or, in the case of *Atom*, by the recently introduced strawberry lift rings.

Mention may also be made of those varieties whose fruit is golden when ripe. They have never gained great popularity, probably because red is the colour one habitually associates with a ripe tomato.

The yellow varieties do not, as a rule, crop so heavily as the red and the fruit is only of medium size, but they are well worth growing for their sweetness and delicate flavour. *Golden Sunrise* is the best known of these yellow varieties.

The scientific breeding of improved varieties is currently the subject of considerable work, notably at the Glasshouse Crops Research Institute, Littlehampton. Superior fruit quality, evenness of ripening, freedom from greenback, resistance to leaf mould and wilt diseases, are some of the important factors being bred into new varieties. *Craigella*, of *Ailsa Craig* parentage, is one such variety. *Moneycross* combines freedom from greenback and resistance to leaf mould with the familiar advantages of *Moneymaker*.

105

Appendix

USEFUL FACTS, FIGURES AND FORMULAE

J.I. Composts

Reference has been made in Chapter 3 to the John Innes Potting Compost (J.I.P.). Most gardeners in these days know all about this compost and many have on their bookshelves the excellent publications on the subject issued by the John Innes Horticultural Institution, who were formerly at Merton, Surrey, thereafter at Bayfordbury, Hertfordshire, and latterly at Norwich. It is often useful, however, to have the essential information about the mixture ready to hand when doubts arise.

There are two and, apart from purely specialist purposes in connection with plants intolerant of lime, only two John Innes composts.

J.I. Seedling Compost (J.I.S.) does not interest us directly since the relatively large-seeded and vigorous tomato does not need to be sown into the milder mixture specially devised for general seed sowing and J.I. Potting Compost (J.I.P.) is entirely satisfactory.

Now the one point, from my experience, which so often confuses the amateur user of this compost is the reference to J.I.P.1, J.I.P.2 and J.I.P.3. It is perhaps reasonable enough to think that these are three fundamentally different mixtures. In fact, however, they are nothing more than the basic mixture of loam, sand and peat to each bushel of which has been added 1, 2 and 3 doses of J.I. base fertilizer and 1, 2 and 3 doses of carbonate of lime. In other words, J.I.P.3 is merely three times as rich in food elements as J.I.P.1, but they both look and are the same physically. Consequently we can call the ideal physical mixture J.I.P. and only add the numbers when the varying amounts of base fertilizer and chalk have been added.

J.I.P. has the following composition:

> 7 parts by volume of sterilized loam
> 3 parts by volume of well-moistened spongy peat
> 2 parts by volume of coarse, sharp sand

I have referred to the desirable characteristics of these three basic materials in Chapter 3 and it is only necessary here to emphasize the need for very thorough mixing of these ingredients.

The best way from my experience is to make up about 3 bushels of J.I.P. at a time. A clean concrete surface is required and the loam, peat and all but a few handfuls of the sand are put down in layers one above the other. It is then simple enough to achieve thorough mixing by turning the whole lot into a heap and re-turning backwards and forwards at least twice.

When all the ingredients seem well mixed the required amount of J.I. Base mixed into the remaining sand is scattered over the flattened heap. The carbonate of lime, if required, is also dusted over and the whole lot turned over again at least twice. As a final insurance against uneven mixing I like to pass the whole lot through a ½-inch sieve.

This may seem like making hard work of a simple job, but it is essential to ensure really thorough mixing. Many of the disappointments with J.I.P. compost at its various fertilizer strengths are undoubtedly due to uneven mixing.

The carbonate of lime, incidentally, is added solely to compensate for the acidifying effects of the base fertilizer. Consequently, the indicated amounts should always be added unless the loam or soil, as the case may be, has been found to have plenty of free lime.

J.I.P.1 involves the addition of ¾ oz. of carbonate of lime and 4 oz. of J.I. base to each bushel of the 7:3:2 mixture. For J.I.P.2 one merely uses twice as much of each (1½ oz. and 8 oz.), and for J.I.P.3 three times as much of each (2¼ oz. carbonate of lime and 12 oz. base).

A bushel is 2,200 cubic inches or just over 1¼ cubic feet. It is also equivalent to 8 gallons, and I find the easiest way to measure out the ingredients on a small scale is in units of 2 gallon bucketfuls. Since one is working in accurate quantities, it is as well to check the bucket for capacity by weighing it first and then running in water until the increase in weight is exactly 20 lb. A mark at the water level then gives a future guide for exactly 2 gallons.

This 2 gallon unit is convenient because 7 buckets of loam, 3 of moist, loose peat and 2 of sand gives a total volume of 24 gallons or 3 bushels, and one can take half or double quantities as required.

Finally, to have the compost in a condition for immediate sowing or potting, the loam or soil should be just barely moist, the sand dry and the peat thoroughly moistened but not sodden. Use J.I.P.1 for sowing and for the potting into 60's, J.I.P.2 for the 48's and J.I.P.3 for the growing-season containers.

Measuring Small Quantities

In making up composts one is concerned with ounces and fractions of an ounce, and it is often difficult to measure these accurately. It can be done on a pair of letter scales, but these are seldom available at the right time. Certainly the quantities must be accurate within quite close limits, and reckoning a level tablespoon as ½ oz. of everything in general is not good enough for our purpose.

To overcome this difficulty I use a small but strong graduated glass measure which is obtainable at a cost of around 10p. from all chemists. There are several separate graduations, but the most useful for our purpose is the teaspoon scale.

The following table gives the graduation equivalent of 1 oz. of the fertilizers required in composts when in normal, dry condition and settled in the measure by gentle tapping.

1 oz. Fertilizer	*Graduation Mark*
	Teaspoons
Sulphate of potash	6
Magnesium sulphate (Epsom salts)	8
Carbonate of lime (finely ground)	10
Superphosphate	10
Hoof and horn meal (J.I. grade)	10
J.I. base	10

From this table, fractions of an ounce of any of the materials can easily be calculated and measured.

As this measure is graduated directly for liquid quantities, it is also most useful for quantities of liquid fertilizers up to 2 fl. oz.

The culinary tablespoon and teaspoon vary so much in capacity that it is essential to use the measure to achieve the necessary degree of accuracy when handling concentrated liquid fertilizers and spray fluids.

Glass Protection for Ring Culture

Reference has been made in Chapter 2 to the use of clamps for constructing lean-to cloches for early protection of ring culture plants grown along a fence or wall. This type is known as the Calvert Cloche Clip and it holds the glass gently yet securely. For our purpose only half of a barn cloche is required, since one sheet of glass stands on the ground and the roof member is held in position by the clamp and can be further supported by a batten secured to the fence or wall at an appropriate height.

Where there may be a risk of these half cloches being blown away from the fence, they can be secured individually by a string run from fence to a peg in the ground or by a string stretched from end to end against the upward sloping face. A suitable size of glass for this purpose is 15 inches square.

The cost of these clips is about 15p. each and they are obtainable from most retailers. From my own experience, these clips are by far the simplest method so far evolved of forming sheets of glass into various types of cloche structure.

Electrical Soil Sterilizer

As mentioned in the chapter on the Container Soil, partial sterilization using electric power as a source of heat is ideal but involves special equipment.

The Camplex model HD 5112 Soil Sterilizer is a thoroughly reliable and safe piece of equipment. The capacity is 1 bushel and the current price about £32. The loading of the heating unit is $1\frac{1}{2}$ kW. and the partial sterilization of a charge of soil is completed in about $1\frac{1}{2}$ hours for an approximate consumption of $2\frac{1}{4}$ units of electricity. The rather high cost of this apparatus is largely offset by the fact that it can also be used as a greenhouse heater. This type, incidentally, involves indirect panel units rather than electrode heating as previously described.

Further details of this equipment, of soil heating cables, irradiator lamps for supplementing the natural light and of low-consumption tubular heaters can be obtained from Simplex of Cambridge Ltd, Sawston, Cambridge.

Appendix

Soil Preparation

By reason of the emphasis on ring culture both in the greenhouse and out of doors, I have omitted any detailed reference to soil preparation in the chapters on Culture. For those, however, who wish to keep to long-established methods, the following notes may be helpful.

The first year after building a new greenhouse the border soil almost invariably produces an excellent crop, at least as far as weight is concerned, with the minimum of treatment. On a heavy soil it is sufficient to incorporate a generous dressing of sphagnum peat—at least 4 gallons loose bulk of the well-moistened material per square yard—and 4–8 oz. per square yard of J.I. Base, according to how generously the land was treated in the year or two prior to the house being built.

On light, sharply drained land, both potash and magnesium tend to be washed down below root level during watering and the dressing of J.I. base should be supplemented with 2 oz. of sulphate of potash and 4 oz. of magnesium sulphate per square yard. Where good quality stable manure in partly rotted condition is available, it can be used instead of the peat though, with silty soils which tend to pack down hard or 'pan' under the influence of water, peat holds the soil in open condition better than manure.

A useful compromise is to use $\frac{1}{2}$ peat and $\frac{1}{2}$ manure to the same total volume per square yard and, if desired, the fresh stable manure can be bulked-up with an equal volume of dry peat and the resulting heap thoroughly watered to provide a peat/manure mixture for use two or three months later.

This same routine can be followed in every detail to prepare the soil for outdoor culture. Practically any type of soil will produce a satisfactory crop when treated in this manner.

Appendix

A change of site each season overcomes any of the troubles which tend to arise where the same crop is grown year after year in the same soil. It is desirable, however, not to plant where potatoes have been since the two crops are closely allied and there are several root-attacking pests and diseases common to both.

In the greenhouse, tomatoes are grown year after year and one has to compensate for the lack of rotation. This can be done either by removing the border soil to the depth of 9 in. or so at the end of each season and replacing with soil from outside or, with less labour but rather less effectively, by sterilizing with formaldehyde. This formaldehyde treatment is carried out when the late chrysanthemums, housed after the tomatoes, are finished and involves applying 5 gallons per sq. yd. of a solution made by diluting 1 pint of the concentrate with 5–6 gallons of water.

The soil should be stirred with a spade during application to ensure complete saturation and penetration, and further solution should be applied if necessary to achieve this condition.

After treatment the soil should be covered with old sacks for a week and then forked over roughly to allow the fumes to escape. A resting period of at least a month is usually needed before the soil is free of formaldehyde vapour and no plants should be put into the house until the test described in an earlier chapter shows complete freedom.

This formaldehyde treatment can be extended to outdoor soil where it is necessary to grow tomatoes by ordinary methods in the same place year after year. The effect is quite good, but it is important not to let the soil become frozen until most of the fumes have escaped. The best way to overcome this is to carry out treatment while the soil is still warm and fairly dry immediately after the season's crop is completed; cover with sacks for a week, fork over roughly and then put down a layer 2 inches thick of dry peat. This allows the fumes to continue escaping, insulates against frost and is ready for digging-in during the spring cultivation.

Finally, a point on applying water to the greenhouse soil during the dormant period. The commercial grower floods heavily—to the extent of a total of 30–50 gallons per square yard in several applications—to take the place of the winter rains which would normally fall on the ground. If this is not done, soluble residues from the base dressings and growing-season feeds accumulate and prevent effective root action. This can be done either before the formaldehyde treatment or once the fumes have fully escaped.

On balance, I advise changing the border soil at least every second year if possible. It is hard work but it avoids the processes of sterilizing and flooding.

Fruit Splitting

It is not unusual for a considerable proportion of fruit to be blemished, and subsequently lost by rotting, due to splitting during the ripening period.

The main cause appears to be a fluctuating supply of water to the fruit and this, in turn, is due to infrequent, heavy waterings which cause the whole plant, including the fruit, to harden during the dry periods. Abundant water supplied to dry roots causes an upsurge of sap and a rapid swelling of previously restricted fruit. The drought-hardened skin of the fruit cannot stretch sufficiently and the sap tension is relieved by splitting.

The answer is to maintain adequate water at the roots—and hence a steady sap-stream—at all times and particularly in hot, dry periods when the leaves are losing water rapidly.

By reason of the provision of a continually moist and well-aerated aggregate, ring culture practically eliminates trouble with splitting.

The other closely, allied, cause is a sudden diversion of the sap-stream from extension growth to the fruit. For this reason, plants stopped when the maximum number of trusses have developed which can be expected to ripen, should be allowed to produce side shoots to draw off the sap. These, in turn, can be stopped at three or four leaves to prevent a wild, overgrown condition.

Hormone Setting

Particularly in the early season under glass, when growth tends to be over-vigorous, setting is often irregular. Much-branched trusses, growing almost vertically rather than bending in a curve outwards from the stem, frequently set badly and carry fruit only on the extremities.

If the bloom colour is pale yellow rather than the desirable golden shade, a teaspoonful of superphosphate per plant carried in by a normal watering often brings about improved setting.

Under such circumstances, however, it is as well also to compensate for the shyness in natural setting by application of a growth-regulatory or 'hormone' preparation. If more than an occasional bloom fades without the appearance of a fruitlet the size of a small pea, the whole truss should be treated with accurately diluted hormone solution. Since each unfertilized pin-point ovary must be wetted but the solution kept off the foliage as much as possible, I prefer to dip each truss into a basin of the solution.

With a little care this can be done effectively and it helps penetration to remove the faded yellow 'petals' before dipping.

The illustration shows hormone-set fruits swelling alongside a normally set fruit. Such fruit may ripen rather small and is seedless. The flavour and texture, however, are normal.

Appendix

Fruit Quality

It is far easier to grow a heavy crop of misshapen, poorly coloured and corky fruit than a medium crop of consistently top quality.

Variety comes prominently into the picture. Thus, *Potentate*, heavily fed with nitrogen, is capable of a very heavy crop but the quality under such circumstances varies from poor to atrocious. On the other hand, *Radio* and kindred varieties give lighter crops of naturally higher quality. Commercially there is still too little premium on quality to justify the lower cropping of the 'smooth' varieties and until the housewife is considerably more critical of what she buys the emphasis will continue to be on weight.

The second factor influencing quality is nutrition. Generally speaking, the ranker the plants the poorer will be the quality of fruit and excess nitrogen relative to potash makes for rank growth. Conversely, a hard 'potash' plant produces small, firm, very sweet and perfectly coloured fruit.

In ordinary soil culture it is difficult to strike the happy medium in growth which gives a fair crop of high quality—which, as amateur growers, is what we want. From my experience, ring culture provides the answer to this quest since it enables a plant to be heavily fed with potash without stunting the growth and reducing the size of fruit unduly.

I find, for example, that *Moneymaker*, a variety intermediate between *Potentate* and *Radio* for cropping and quality, gives a good crop under ring culture even though the highest quality is sought by giving straight sulphate of potash feeds alternately with those of 667 at the early fruiting stages. This is well demonstrated by the details of my own 1955 season crops both in the greenhouse and out of doors. The weight was certainly there, yet it was difficult to find a fruit which was not perfect in colour and texture.

115

Appendix

Poor quality fruit is not worthy of our time and bother no matter how heavy the crop. Given plenty of potash, adequate magnesium, and the opportunity to ripen to a full red colour on the plant, the tomato ceases to be a mere vegetable and becomes a fruit in every sense.

Physical Condition of Fertilizers

Where one is employing small quantities of various fertilizers, as in preparing J.I. composts, it is most important for the sake of uniformity that all lumps be broken down. Thus, with superphosphate and sulphate of potash, I always pass a quantity through a household flour sieve (originally 'acquired' and since retained for this purpose!) before measuring or weighing. Carbonate of lime should always be bought in finely ground condition—crushed limestone is relatively useless for our purpose—while magnesium sulphate is sold in fine, crystalline form which does not become lumpy. J.I. Base sometimes sets rather solid and this is best rubbed between the hands before measuring as a flour sieve holds back much of the hoof and horn which is intentionally present as $\frac{1}{8}$th inch particles.

Greenhouse Insulation

An established development in greenhouse culture is the use of thin, pliable, light-transparent plastic film fixed inside the house to the glazing bars to provide an insulating air-lock. The sheets of film, usually 38 inches or 50 inches wide, are overlapped to the extent of 2 inches or so and are fixed in taut condition to the bars by means of special wire staples or with drawing pins. Ventilators are lined separately so that they can be opened and shut as usual.

The effect of lining a house is to exclude draughts and to cut down heat losses to a very marked degree. Critical trials have shown that a temperature advantage of as much as 15° F. can be gained, the source of heat and all other factors remaining constant. This means, of course, that one can either hold a higher temperature in the house with an existing heating unit or hold the same temperature with a smaller unit. The fact that the entry of sun heat is checked to the same extent as loss of artificial heat from within, means that a more even temperature is maintained in a lined house and this is always a desirable circumstance.

The special sheeting used for this purpose is impermeable to water vapour and consequently a very high humidity can be maintained. This is excellent at the propagating and early season growth periods, but as the season advances and leaf mould and Botrytis diseases become prevalent I have found it necessary to remove the lining from the walls and ends of the house and retain only the roof lining to check the sun glare and thus act as light shading.

An illustration shows this sheeting on the upper portion of my own house. As the framework of this house is metal the sheeting had to be stuck on with a latex cement. By careful manipulation the result was well worth while, but another time I shall erect a skeleton wood-batten framework inside to facilitate fixing and to allow a more effective air-gap between sheeting and glass. This temporary double-glazing of greenhouses has great possibilities and, from my own experience to date, I can thoroughly recommend it.

Cloche Culture

There is a considerable literature on the use of cloches for the early season culture of both garden and market crops, and tomatoes figure widely as an obvious example of a subject which benefits by such protection.

Where, for one reason or another, it is not convenient to

Appendix

grow against the shelter of a wall, fence or some improvised structure, it is possible to grow a fairly early crop in the open garden or allotment with the aid of barn-type cloches.

Soil preparation follows the lines indicated earlier in this section and, since most gardeners are conversant with the use of cloches and there are, as stated above, ample references on the subject, I have no need to elaborate in great detail. The following are, however, points particularly worth noting.

Planting can take place nearly as early as where background shelter is available, and early May is a fair indication for the southern half of the country. It is an advantage to plant in a trench 3 or 4 inches deep sloping up towards the side glass since additional protection is thus afforded and the increased head room allows the cloches to be kept over the plants for a week or so longer.

If this shallow-trench method is adopted with heavy soil, it is very desirable to work in a good dressing of coarse, sharp sand and also to surround the neck of each plant with sand to overcome any tendency to stagnant moisture.

Usually for the first three weeks or so little or no ventilation will be required but gradually, by allowing a space between each cloche, more and more air is given. Experience is the only sound guide in this matter and due regard must be paid to the prevailing weather. Thus, it might be possible, and indeed desirable, to allow some ventilation in mid-May while at the end of the month a sudden cold spell would dictate a return to maximum protection.

The cloches duly spaced as required for ventilation can be retained as a covering until the foliage reaches the glass; thereafter the cloches can be turned on end to give continued protection to the lower trusses from cold winds.

The usual routine of feeding, pest and disease control and of hormone spraying for setting applies as described in earlier chapters.

118

Appendix

For those interested to carry this system one stage further, a soil-heating cable can be laid beneath the plants to provide the warm root-run so desirable for quick establishment. Where this is done it will usually be found fully adequate to use heat only at night as a reserve of warmth is thus built up and over-heating with consequent soft growth is avoided.

From my experience, a wide range of varieties give good results by this system, including the bush tomatoes such as *Amateur*, but I personally still prefer *Moneymaker*.

Spacing of the plants beneath the cloches will depend to some extent upon the variety, but on the average one plant set beneath the centre of each cloche is a good arrangement.

Finally, the cloches can be returned to service to help in ripening off the fruit in an unfavourable autumn. For this purpose the plants are cut down from the supporting stakes, the leaves removed and the bines laid along the row with the fruit resting on a bed of dry straw or peat. With the cloches again covering the row some heat is trapped and ripening promoted.

Carbon Dioxide (CO$_2$) Enrichment of the Glasshouse Atmosphere

It has for long been known that many plants and, in particular, tomatoes and cucumbers benefit in respect of growth rate and fruit production if the atmosphere around them is enriched with CO$_2$ up to around threefold of the natural level.

Only of recent years, however, have the various sources of CO$_2$ become sufficiently cheap to permit economic enrichment. Commercial growers are currently employing this means towards more profitable growing to a considerable and increasing degree.

One method of enrichment is to install in the house special lamps burning propane gas. Lamps of this type are currently advertised in the gardening press for use in the amateur greenhouse. In view of the fact, however, that the effective uptake of

119

additional CO_2 by the plants is not efficient at temperatures much below 65 degrees—well above the temperature to which amateurs habitually heat their greenhouse—I do not consider this enrichment to be a very practical or economic proposition under our circumstances.

Experience shows that any advantages obtainable from artificial CO_2 enrichment are also achieved to a substantial degree by employing the straw-bale method of culture detailed in Chapter 6. It will be noted that CO_2 is given off in the course of the slow decomposition of the straw, so any advantages from increased CO_2 are obtained without additional cost or bother of installing special apparatus.

INDEX

121

Index

Index

Index